THE BLIND DATE

The Missing Link To Bridal Readiness

Michelle Maddox

The Blind Date, The Missing Link To Bridal Readiness

Published by About Face Books

ISBN: 979-8-9943873-0-6

Book Design by Sabryna Washington

TABLE OF CONTENTS

Eye Opening Preface To Our Blind Date With Christ The King

What God is currently doing has been a hidden message until He told me to write this book and release His message. It is a message that defies logic. What I mean when I say that is..... our minds are where all intelligence and understanding reside, OUR MINDS ARE LOGICAL. Our minds are fallen and cursed because of the event in the garden when Adam and Eve ate the fruit of the tree of the knowledge of good and evil.

When they ate of the tree, satan planted doubt in Eve's mind when he asked her, "did God really mean don't eat of this tree?"

She took that seed of doubt and questioned God's original intention for us.

THE ORIGINAL INTENTION FOR US IS TO HAVE MINDS CREATED FROM THE FOUNDATION OF THE EARTH WITHOUT THE FALL OF MANKIND. PERFECT MINDS. NOT FALLEN AND CURSED MINDS PRODUCED WITH ADAM AND EVE EATING OF THE TREE.

This is because in the foundation of the Earth there existed the Father, the Son, and the Holy Spirit. ALL of mankind was created with a perfect mind of perfection and glory in the foundations of the Earth. That includes us. ALL OF MANKIND! This is called God's original intention.

His original intention was for OUR minds, which is the same thing as our souls, to be perfect, complete, whole, not fallen and cursed. NOT LOGICAL AND ANALYTICAL.

His original intention was for us to have perfected minds of glory without any form of mental struggles, FEARS, addictions, judgments, opinions, attitudes, religious strongholds, denominations and even sicknesses.

His original intention was a mind created in His glory without all the aspects which make us opinionated, persuaded outside of His perfect will, and drawn to all kinds of confusion and darkness. **The fall of mankind produced a fallen mind, which is a mind cursed with confusion and analytical reasoning. Including our understanding of WHO HE IS!**

His original intention, also including that perfection, was to take place in Adam and Eve rather than a cursed and fallen mind. God Himself walked with them in the garden of Genesis. He walked with them personally. A PERSONAL CONNECTION OF PERFECTED LIFE IN HIM! God's original intention was that they would grow to be perfected, not fallen and cursed. PERFECTED IN HIS LIFE!

WHAT MOST PEOPLE DON'T REALIZE, BECAUSE OF OUR LIMITED AND CURSED MINDS, IS THAT CHRIST THE KING WAS ALSO IN THE FOUNDATIONS OF THE EARTH. AND HERE'S THE REAL TRUTH THAT OFFENDS MOST PEOPLE...

JESUS WAS GOD'S PLAN B.

GOD SENT JESUS TO BE OUR SAVIOR AS YOU WELL KNOW, BUT HE HAD TO DO THAT BECAUSE ADAM AND EVE MESSED UP GOD'S ORIGINAL PLAN. THEY MESSED UP HIS ORIGINAL INTENTION.

PRODUCING OUR NEED TO BE SAVED FROM THE FALL OF MANKIND.

It was NOT God's original plan to send a Savior. But the fall of mankind created the need for a Savior and God sent us the BEST SAVIOR OF JESUS.

BUT IT IS TIME FOR CHRIST THE KING!

The book is about a blind date with Christ the King of Redemption, who was created along with us in the foundations of the Earth with God's ORIGINAL INTENTION OF HOW HE WANTED THINGS TO BE.

Jesus of Nazareth did a perfect job. He was fully God and fully man BUT HE WAS LIMITED BY GOD.

JUST LIKE WE HAVE BEEN LIMITED BY OUR CURSED MINDS.

Now, Jesus DID NOT have a cursed mind. He was without sin! But God limited what Jesus could do and that is why Jesus said we would do greater works than He did!

The book is about Christ the King of Redemption, God's original intention created in the foundations of the Earth at the very beginning, NOW COMING FORTH TO CHANGE EVERYTHING BEGINNING WITH OUR MINDS.

It's the vastness of Christ we HAVE NEVER KNOWN.

ITS ABOUT THE CHRIST SINCE THE FOUNDATIONS OF THE EARTH WHO HAS BEEN ON HOLD BECAUSE JESUS HAD TO COME FIRST AND BE OUR SAVIOR.

NOW ITS TIME FOR CHRIST THE KING OF REDEMPTION!!

AND THAT'S WHY WE HAVE TO LAY ASIDE JESUS OF NAZARETH WHO GOT US THIS FAR!

IT IS SO WE CAN EMBRACE CHRIST THE KING OF REDEMPTION, GOD'S ORIGINAL INTENTION!

And it offends the fallen mind of man because HE is speaking of the Mind of Christ which contains THE VASTNESS OF WHO HE REALLY IS!

The 'Blind Date' is getting to know HIS vastness we have never known, hence a blind date. GETTING TO KNOW THE GREAT I AM!

The 'Missing Link' is allowing Christ the King to replace Jesus of Nazareth who got us this far!! We would not be this far without Jesus of Nazareth.

THE CURSED MIND OF MAN IS LOGICAL. THE MIND OF CHRIST DEFIES LOGIC. IT IS NOT LOGICAL.

THEREFORE, THE BOOK MUST BE READ BY PRAYING AND ASKING HIM TO OPEN THE MIND OF CHRIST AS WE READ.

You are invited to read every word and every page with the Mind of Christ overriding
the fallen and cursed mind of man so that you too, may go on a blind date with CHRIST THE KING OF REDEMPTION!

HE IS WORTHY OF IT ALL!!

Chapter 1
Vital To Read Before You Begin

He is for <u>You</u> To Be Made Ready.

The true fun and excitement, the true Bridal growth of readiness found in these writings, begins to take place in chapter 5. However, I STRONGLY encourage you to press through the very brief chapters of 1-4 so you will have the matrix and groundwork of where we are headed.

HE IS FOR US TO BE MADE READY!!!!

Upfront, I want to make it very clear, the writings put together in this book are not informing us of what He is going to do in the near or far away future. They are about what HE IS currently and actively doing of which we must participate and catch up with HIM!

Also, I want to stress, stress, stress these writings are out of His Love we don't even know. He is beginning to expose His Love to me and pour it out regarding His Heart for His Bride to know Him as Christ, the King of Redemption, rather than Jesus of Nazareth. Nothing I have written is purposely intended to be haughty or brassy. It's all passion for us as His Bride to individually, really grasp and never let go of how passionately in love He is with us and how passionately ready He is for us to also be ready.

Some of chapters 1-4, because of being read from printed words on paper pages could very well come across as indeed brassy, sassy, and haughty. But God's heart, the heart of Christ, and my heart are none of those things. The heart in these writings is pure, raw, transparency of where He is coming from, where I am coming from, and why He has chosen me to write the words that fill these pages.

I do personally know some who will be reading these pages. However, most of those who will be reading, I do not know and have never met. But I want you to know that because of the LOVE of Christ, I do love you all. Because you are also a Bride being made ready, I love you dearly.

Overall this is a “disclaimer” of sorts. I am not a writer. I am doing this simply because the Lord‘s hand has been strong on me to do it. Be warned now these writings do not flow from chapter to chapter the way a typical book reads where each chapter backs up and continues the previous chapter. These chapters all address the need for the Bride to get ready, however, they were written independently and not written to flow.

Also, the content of these chapters is extremely repetitive. He has a specific intention as to why they are so repetitive. I encourage you not to stop reading because you’ve already read something multiple times. Continue because throughout the repetitiveness there are nuggets and treasures and it is all from Him. I simply put it on paper for the corporate bride.

He was showing me even as I was writing this very first part of the book, He is very passionate for His Bride. He is ready. He showed me internally that He is already standing at the altar, waiting for His chosen Bride. Therefore, He is passionately reaching out to us with a very specific purpose because time is running out. We have all been in a process of self surrender for years now. You will soon read this book is about the missing link of another level of surrender He is looking for in order for us to be ready to meet Him at the altar.

He let me know the pattern of repetition in these writings is designed to force the deeper surrender. Like knocking on a door over and over.

You will also be reading quite a bit about the missing link of readiness which specifically is the annihilation of the fallen mind of man unto the Mind of Christ, which is redemption. As I finished up this book and read over it myself, I questioned

Him as to all the repetition and He clearly let me know the repetitions in and of themselves are annihilations to combat the fallen mind. His agenda is for the fallen mind of man to surrender to the annihilations in this book, including the repetitions.

He is Mount Zion. The altar where He is standing, waiting for His Bride is at the very top of Mount Zion. He is waiting for us. Longing and waiting and looking for us. Some of us He can already clearly see. Some of us He is still calling to climb up. But He wants us to know it's time to climb the mountain with a dedicated and fierce focus.

Regarding the repetitions, He was showing me that when we climb a natural mountain, it is step, after step, after step, after step, after step, after step. A repetition of steps. A repetition of walking, and walking again, and walking again. A repetition of climbing, climbing higher, climbing higher, and climbing higher.

It is the same with the repetitions in this book. They are specifically designed by HIM as taking steps up Mount Zion to meet Him at the altar. Repetition, after repetition, after repetition, after step, after step, after step. Repetition to get us to the top, and repetition to annihilate along the way. And in the same way climbing a physical mountain gets weary and we get tired of another step, and another step, and another step, there is a specific goal in mind.

He has a specific goal for us in these writings with these repetitions.

Hang in there, Dear Bridal Friends! It's all about surrender. A deeper surrender. A missing link of a very specific surrender.

He calls the mountain peak of the test of deeper surrender, His checkmate. His checkmate is the victory point!

He is our Prince of Peace, our Counselor, our Mighty God! He is for us, longing for us, and letting us know exactly where we are lacking, so we can focus on the repetitive steps and make it to the top to join Him!

The book is not a book to read for entertainment, it is a book to read for equipping. He is speaking to each of us because time is short, and He is being repetitively insistent to get the message across.

I do not apologize for the repetitiveness, however, I am mentioning it because He has made it very clear to me it is for His very intentional reasons. Just push through and keep going. If you press on through these writings, you will find His purpose.

I believe in you. I am pulling for you. This was written specifically and intentionally for you. If each of us, each of His individual and chosen Bride will surrender to the truth He has shared with me which I have shared in these pages, before we can turn around and scream, Come Lord, Come! He will be here for us!!

Every word in these pages is built from a matrix of love above all other foundations of which I will share in chapters one through four.

Please know you are valuable, you are chosen, and you are dearly and passionately loved!

We all inherited, from the garden with Adam and Eve, the fall of mankind. We all inherited by default, the fallen and cursed mind of man that operates strictly from intelligence and fallen understanding. None of these pages, and none of these words will do the work of readiness if we read them and process them through this fallen and cursed mind. The fallen mind is the LOGICAL MIND OF MAN. It is the logical mind that insist everything "make sense". It is the mind that reasons things out. **NOTHING IN THESE PAGES IS LOGICAL. IT ALL DEFIES LOGIC. Every aspect of it. EVERYTHING IN THESE PAGES RESIDES IN THE MIND OF CHRIST.**

We must read and process these printed words through the Mind of Christ He is currently and sovereignly releasing. You will read more about this sovereign move as you continue. For currently He is sovereignly releasing the Mind of Christ. If the beautiful truth of redemption and the beautiful truth of our remaining readiness shared in this book are not read and processed through the Mind of Christ, the outcome will be great offense, bondage, and a lack of readiness that will stop us dead in our tracks.

We must read and process these words through the beautifully and sovereignly available Mind of Christ. **The Mind of Christ is where the knowings of Christ reside and from which they are released.** That is an important sentence. So I will repeat it again. The Mind of Christ is where the knowings of Christ reside and from which they are released. Therefore, I am going to pray this over each of us before we even go a step farther......

"Christ the King of Redemption we praise you, we honor you, we glorify you, for you are the King we long for! We ask for the Mind of Christ to sovereignly open up over every reader, over every word, over every sentence, over every paragraph, over every chapter, so that your perfect, divine, and sovereign will come forth at this very moment and take place in each individual reading what you are writing on these pages. We thank you that you love us so much you have not only ordained the sovereign time of the Mind of Christ and of full redemption unto the Mind of Christ, but you also ordained the sovereign time and moment of the bridal truths in this small book. And you sovereignly as

well chose the God ordained readers of these pages. We corporately lean in with hunger. We corporately thank you and praise you. We corporately say yes and amen to your true heart and mind of what you are after that we have yet to embrace so we are a Bride made ready. So to you, Lord, we corporately say come, Lord come, and open The Mind of Christ over us. Come, Lord come and redeem us. Wake us up to what has held us back and have your ready Bride. We love you Lord and we are grateful you have counted us worthy to make it all the way to you, the Bridegroom about to have His Bride. We praise you! We anxiously await seeing you face to face. Amen!"

Together, let's get this readiness complete so we can be called to CHRIST THE KING OF REDEMPTION!!

This book was written in the format of personal journaling, notations, thoughts, and processes through encounters with the Life of Christ leading us into full redemption of the Mind of Christ. It was not written by a published author or by applying any proper rules of how to assemble a book, pages, paragraphs, etc.

- **It is not properly edited, refined, or defined.**
- **But it is a gift.**

The above statements are to help you navigate the rawness of these pages. I have found it more important to finish these writings and to assemble much of what I have done in the last four years in a prompt manner and get it to you without the worry and concerns of the establishment, or any expectations of man or book publishing rules, rights, wrongs or publishing companies. Including proper wording, punctuation, running sentences, paragraphs, and "all the things" involved in both writing and editing a book.

The Lord has laid this on my heart to get done now. In a timely manner. Editing takes massive amounts of collective hours. With the statement of "now", I am not stating we don't have time to do this or read this set of writings before He calls His Bride to Him and sends her back. For whatever reason of His, He has just made it clear to "get it done now". I am not using the word or the timeframe of "now" to imply a timeframe of when He will be responding to a Bride made ready. Therefore, due to Him telling me to do this "now", content is taking precedence over exactness of editing details.

It has not been, nor will it be perfectly edited. It is simply being assembled, produced, and distributed.

Let Christ guide you through these powerful truths while overlooking the casual assembly of these pages.

Lastly, scripture references are seldom referred to and in most cases they are not listed or included. You can add those if you prefer.

Hang in there! Reading and consuming these writings might get challenging at times due to the content, but if consumed properly through HIS LIFE and allowing HIM to speak to You beyond the words on these pages, you will come out at the end of the book UNDONE for HIM.

These writings are to be a wake up call into His life. And they are to be a funeral of self life.

These writings are to offend so much OUT of us. And, these writings are to birth so much IN to us.

These writings are to challenge you and make you so mad and motivated they catapult you into the truth of His Life and into the depths of His Bosom where He is truly taking His Bride.

Nothing I have written in this chapter is insecurity, an apology, or an excuse. These writings are exactly what He wants them to be. I tried to rearrange and redo things, but He put His hand on me to stop. Therefore, I trust His purpose, not only in the truths of these writings, but in the format as well.

These writings will be a blessing. And these writings will be a curse UNTIL you see the curse lies within the fallen mind, causing the delay of our corporate readiness.

This is a short book of only a taste of what He has served. **It is intentionally short so you can eat it, digest it, live it, and become it.**

The meal He is serving is hot and ready on the table to be eaten in a timely manner because time as we know it is very, very short. The time of readiness is short, although I wouldn't dare to guess the exactness of the time.

The message in these writings is not saying the Bride has been wrong or that you individually are wrong in your walk. The message is of the missing link we have overlooked. It comes at the end of the process we have all been in.

It is NOW time for THE MISSING LINK of the THE BLIND DATE.

Come Lord, Come!

NOTES

NOTES

Chapter 2
Introduction

Eat it. Drink it. <u>Become</u> the Truth of the Christ of Redemption.

This book is written for those who do not just want more of Christ, but want all of Christ. The truth within this book, the truth of Christ the King, are sovereignly on hold for the generational blessing of Abraham, Isaac, and Jacob released unto us. It is for us, our children, and our grandchildren, for He is currently working in the generational blessing of three generations.

Not only to be received and flowing throughout three generations, but including that third generation of children, even very young children. The manchild has already been found in the Earth, and there is no age limit of how old or how young within these three generations. Even very young children are hearing the voice of the Life of Christ in the internal and knowing exactly what HE is currently saying and doing.

It is for those who are not only desperate for all of Him, but are also living dangerous enough to embrace all of Him. We must be desperate and dangerous to even embrace the truth of a Christ we have yet to know. And more desperate to LIVE the reality of His original intention in the creation of the Earth. He wants us desperate enough to absolutely embrace that we were created to have the Mind of Christ rather than the cursed and fallen mind of man we inherited from the garden and the actions of Adam and Eve.

This book will be offensive. It will offend the fallen and cursed mind of man that is set against the Mind of Christ. However, with each offense, HE is our breakthrough into the mind of Christ, which is the true and unadulterated love of God, the government of Heaven, the sevenfold spirits of God, the true Christ of Redemption.

This book is about the beautiful exchange from fallenness into redemption. The exchange is scathingly hard and abundantly annihilating, but totally worth it and sovereignly

being offered to us at this time.

The words on these pages will offend everything not of Him. For most of what we have is not truly of Him. The words on these pages will offend religion, traditions of men, rules and regulations. Everything we have known of Him. These words will offend because He is releasing the truth of the vastness of who HE TRULY is of which we have never known. When we are introduced to the unknown, it offends.

So hold on. Keep reading. Don't quit. Don't give up. Because in doing so you are chancing a disqualification of the greatest show on Earth.

His sovereignty has been released and is being offered to us in this time through the gift of complete redemption of the Mind of Christ, replacing the fallen and cursed mind of Man we all inherited.

This book is a rare treasure.

In writing the beautiful truths of this book that do indeed qualify it as a treasure, no attempt has been made to explain or to manipulate any logical sense from the things God has revealed of the Mind of Christ. Because in doing so, that would be applying the fallen cursed mind over the beauty of the Mind of Christ, such as spreading a layer of mud over a diamond.

Therefore, when you do not understand something with the fallen mind we all currently possess, surrender it unto the Mind of Christ and let Him bring Himself, which is the Mind of Christ into your internal space and allow HIM to reveal HIMSELF to YOU on this blind date! **Eat it. Drink it. Become the TRUTH of THE CHRIST OF REDEMPTION.**

Now let's continue.....

NOTES

NOTES

Chapter 2
Excuse Me, Please!

On the other side of offense, is the breakthrough of Him.

THESE WRITINGS ARE NOT ABOUT ME.

I find it very important we start from the beginning just clarifying and getting out of the way who I am as well as why I will at times refer to myself in these writings. I have found it to be way more validating for the reader to know the things I am sharing, I have also actually lived and are currently living. This writing is not a combination or even a culmination of ideas, thoughts, theories, or even promises of God. They are actual realities that have taken place and are currently taking place in my life and in the lives of others.

I titled this chapter EXCUSE ME, PLEASE because this book/writing is not 'about' me at all. Although at times I will refer to myself, my life, and my encounters with Christ, it is not in any way 'about' ME. I am merely one of the vessels in whom and through whom Christ is doing the things I am sharing.

Furthermore, I will share the following of myself so you know as you go deeper, the matrix from which I am writing. There again, not about me at all, but about what He is currently doing that is available for any of His people who are willing to surrender their existence of self unto the fullness of His perfect existence.

I am a woman. From the south. I am called to ministry. I am an apostle/prophet. I don't mind being that honest and vulnerable that I am an apostle, and I am a prophet. The Lord told me years ago, ***"let them know who I am forming you to be so they will know which part of my heart they are receiving from."***

And guess what? Every mature Bride who has survived this far in the readiness process, particularly those who will make it all the way, are also apostle/prophet. For the Bride He is making ready and about to call to Himself is His mature creation of apostle/prophet. So, hello. Welcome to the team.

The things God has spoken through me over the years have been about HIM and HIS LIFE. Not about people and their possessions. I always called the prophetic words, "utterances of Him". They spoke of HIM and HIS LIFE. They spoke of His perfect will in His vessels. They spoke of His plan of redemption. They spoke of annihilations of Himself to introduce the vastness of who He truly is. They spoke of a love that will do more than we thought His power would do, and so much more! In hindsight when I look back at the utterances of Him spoken over the last years, I can clearly see He was leading us into the direction of a very sovereign move He is currently making. I use the past tense word of 'spoken' because He has already shifted from speaking corporate prophetic truths and corporate utterances of HIMSELF into what we will discuss in another chapter of speaking words that create rather than prophetic words that come with a time of 'wait'.

His new voice is a voice of CREATE, replacing the time period of WAIT!

I am a Bride being made ready. Even His chosen and elite people talk about how the new breed of apostles and prophets are going to be so confrontational, so uprooting, and so scathingly offensive. But when these vessels show up, they are accused of being straight from the pit of hell because of operating in confrontation that uproots and is indeed scathingly offensive. **As a corporate body, we beg and wait for God to make ready the new breed of apostle and prophet, but when they show up the results are drastic. Because He is a sovereign God, He is already perfecting these apostles and prophets who He will use to jerk His corporate body into His perfect will. But when these vessels of the new breed show up, they are so extremely confrontational and offensive, we rebuke them in the name of the Lord.**

We cry out to God for them and then when HE sends them, we rebuke them right out the door. I have lived it over and over and over.

Years ago, the Lord spoke to me, and said, ***"As you continue to grow in me, walk with me, and speak as me, my own people WHO DO NOT KNOW ME will call you Jezebel because of the scathing confrontations I AM REQUIRING to make my Bride ready."***

That has been so very true.

I share all the above to invite you to be careful not to rebuke what the corporate Bride has been asking HIM for.

I do not preach from the pattern of the scriptures. I preach, teach, share, and write from the internal voice of HIS LIFE.

We are not waiting on Christ. He is waiting on us to line up with His offensive ways of getting the job done. He is waiting on us to have no more religion, because religion is a major roadblock to redemption.

I like to say He has resorted to His most scathing measures because time is swiftly running out for those of us who claim we want to be ready for Him. Due to the very small remaining time, He is calling all the shots and He is calling them according to His terms. Most who have wanted all along for Christ to make them ready will now decide what they had signed up for is not what they thought. This is because He knows, already knows, those who will go all the way with Him and who will allow this last stretch of the way, be the most beautiful stretch while also being the most offensive stretch.

The most beautiful thing we need to grasp is that the confrontations or anything harsh, are not intended for those of us who have indeed truly surrendered self without our input to His process. Most offensive confrontations are for the rebellious, the hypocrites, the players, the pretenders. Those who take Him for granted, and sometimes for those truly of Him who are procrastinating and lagging behind. But overall the offensive confrontations are for the rebellious, the pretenders, those who need to be excused from the room so the rest of us can move forward without any leaven spoiling the whole bunch.

The remaining group of those who will be confronted in offensive ways are those of His true Bride, who are not willing to let Him annihilate Jesus of Nazareth to the point that history is nothing more than a fable so he can bring in Christ the King of Redemption. If you found that highly offensive, these writings will confront even you. But push through because the writings contained in this collection are indeed the MISSING LINK to the still lacking readiness of His chosen Bride.

When the offensive confrontations do indeed apply to those of us sincerely allowing Him to make us ready, please know He is confronting with His life, the remaining religion, opinions of man, fear, satan's weapon of doubt, and any tightly gripping self that gets us distracted along the way. Including our grip of self that won't let Jesus of Nazereth annihilate even HIMSELF!!

HE IS THE ONE DOING IT!! HE IS ANNIHILATING HIMSELF, and in the process it annihilates our fallen and cursed mind.

I am finding the biggest hindrances to the Bride not being totally made ready at this point are religion and doubt. Religion encompasses opinions, traditions, rules, and regulations, denial, and so much more. And doubt is the absolute seed of satan if not uprooted, grows and takes over producing a tree, hence a vessel of satan rather than a tree, a vessel of the Life of Christ.

Religion is a roadblock to readiness. Doubt is a death blow

to readiness.

He is here to remove every root of both religion and doubt REGARDING WHO HE TRULY IS ABOUT TO INTRODUCE HIMSELF TO BE, AS CHRIST THE KING OF REDEMPTION!!

Doubt is dangerous and deadly. And HE WILL CONFRONT ANY DOUBT STANDING IN YOUR WAY!

I have indeed seen Him take some of His top chosen and put them in a very confrontational and scathing timeout to get them lined up with Him, remove ALL DOUBT, and then put them back in the race. So I encourage you not to assume corrections and confrontations are only for the rebellious. They are also for his people when needed.

Overall, my most favorite mode of which He is working, is that He's getting His Bride ready with His Life! His Life of joy, peace, the love of God. True beauty for the nasty ashes of self. His main mode of operation for the sincere Bride getting ready is not another sermon on how we are failing. Get that out of here. We have had enough of that fruitless method.

His main mode of operation is constantly breathing His Life in the internal of His Bride to form her into His likeness. He used His life breath in the garden, and He is currently using it now in the internal of His vessels to not only make them ready, but to transform them to reveal Himself to the nations of this Earth.

He told me at least 25 years ago that He was going to use me to *"prime the pump"*. These writings are the priming of the pump and trust me, the first water that comes out is murky, dark, muddy, and yucky. The longer we let the pump run, the cleaner the water gets, and we arrive a Bride made ready.

I have been in ministry of some form or fashion for the last 22 years as of this writing in late 2025. My reputation is brassy and sassy. Highly confrontational. I have been known to kick you out and lead you to the door myself while saying 'get the hell out of here'. Not cussing at all, but literally cleansing the room or the gathering of pure hell. And if it is not needed to be personally lead out the door, I will offend you so deeply you leave on your own before I need to lead you out by the hand.

I am gifted with His Life to offend you, not to comfort you, for His offenses are His design to qualify each of us for the sovereign move He is currently making.

I am one of the new breed.

HOWEVER, THE NEW BREED ARE MESSENGERS WHO ARE AS OFFENSIVE AS THE MESSAGE OF HIM THEY CARRY FORTH TO HIS BRIDE.

THE MESSENGERS ARE AS OFFENSIVE AS THE MESSAGE.

He has told me this new breed along with Himself ***"is more like a Gandalf! More like a TRUE WARRIOR!!"***

I invite you to be so desperate for all of Him that you allow HIM to offend you in these writings because on the other side of offense, is the breakthrough of HIM! ALL OF HIM!! The breakthrough of REDEMPTION!

Now, before you go, any farther, I want to say very loudly and boldly...

You are welcome!

You are welcome for every word in these pages, but ultimately you are welcome that if you allow HIM to fortify you with HIS LIFE, these writings will take you from where you are to where both you and He have been longing for you to reside. You will no longer have the MISSING LINK OF READINESS. You will have readiness in Him!

He wants you to know who you are. You are in line to be His sovereign, chosen vessel of redemption.

And for that, you are welcome!

Regarding the last things I want to share and to get out of the way before we get started are as follows. I am NOT claiming to be the only person who has suffered the following things. I am not a suffering poster child or crisis martyr. I am well aware many, if not most of us have been through the same or similar hardships and trials. But I am sharing mine not only to share where I'm coming from, and for pure transparency of my walk with HIM, but to share some of what I have survived to establish the matrix from which my walk with Christ has been laid.

I want you to know that I have already been, for the last 40 years of my current 65 1/2 years called confused, a failure, mentally ill, wicked, evil, Jezebel, a blatant cauldron stirring witch, haughty, prideful, unrepentant, a vessel of satan, and straight from the pit of hell. I have been kicked out of many churches and personal relationships just for speaking simple truth. No exaggeration. Just for speaking simple truth that challenges those in control.

I'm not aware of anything a reader of these writings could call me that I have not already lived. I am currently married to my third husband, I have moved so many times I have lost count, I have lost more dear friends who I thought were truly friends than I can even recall, and my truthful confrontation that is nothing but pure love has caused me a grievous separation from one of my children, including grandchildren. Of everything the confrontations of Christ has cost me, needless to say that has been the hardest so far. But He is beautifully and eternally faithful, and already in the process of restoring what His confrontations produced due to personal offenses never surrendered for His truth. HE is so very faithful!

Not only is this writing not about me, none of the above has ever been about me, my wants, my wishes or my desires. It has been about HIM lovingly, and also scathingly, reaching out with a desperate grasp for His bride to come out of anything and everything standing between her and her Bridegroom, Christ the King of Redemption.

If we love ourselves, our reputation, and our stuff more than His people He so desires to snatch out of deception, confusion, doubt, and darkness of all kinds, then we are not worthy of His kingdom. I have lost all I had more than once and suffered greatly for being willing to do HIS "dirty work" to confront HIS CHOSEN SO THEY WONT FIND THEMSELVES DISQUALIFIED. All to be grossly accused and rejected. I have read His Word many times and I am well aware that I am in good company with Christ himself as many of you most likely also are for the sad rejections of His people. Those HE loves who are more in love with their agendas than HIS TRUTH.

Every offense He had me speak, every confrontation He had me stand in, every truth He had me offer that became labeled a misunderstanding twisted by the fallen and cursed mind of man, has been the attempt from the fire blazing in His eyes for the Bride He has longed for and is currently calling directly into His Bosom.

It was only a few months ago, at the beginning of 2025 the Lord cleared all that up for me in a time when I was also thinking I had failed THE ONE who matters, the Redeemer of my soul.....

He said TO ME, ...***"I began annihilating your personal life***

over 30 years ago, so that when it was my sovereign time to annihilate myself with the truth of the vastness of who I am on this BLIND DATE, the annihilations of ME prior played out in your life by MY HAND did not offend you, but rather they prepared you to embrace THE ANNIHILATED CHRIST all the way to My Bosom of REDEMPTION".

He was saying to me that He annihilated my personal life and my mind so it was prepared, palatable, ready to receive, and moreso ready to BELIEVE and embrace the annihilations of Himself and the introduction of Christ, the King of Redemption who replaces Jesus of Nazareth. Later in these pages, I will share with you how the Christ of Redemption coming forth very soon for His ready bride absolutely is no longer Jesus of Nazareth.

Of all the things He has spoken to me, that is absolutely one of my most favorites because HE gave purpose to what the church, friends, some family, and relationships of all dynamics has called hell in regards to how my life has looked and how it has played out. He gave HIS purpose to what has been a continuous wrecking ball of my personal life and what man calls failure, defeat, confusion, and my favorite label of "unstable."

His divine and sovereign purpose was able to come forth from a life of personal annihilations so HE COULD PRESENT HIMSELF ANNIHILATED.

Needless to say, religion has been confronted head on in this chapter alone.

I encourage you to read on. Chapter after chapter. And finish. When you are finished, leave your opinions out of the way. And move forward with Him because He already knows who you are, and He is already waiting for your response to the words on these pages.

HE KNOWS THE VERY MOMENT YOU WILL RESPOND AND SAY 'YES AND AMEN' TO THE TRUTHS OF HIM ON THESE PAGES.

HE ALREADY KNOWS THE VERY MOMENT YOU WILL WITH MUCH EXCITEMENT EMBRACE AND HOLD ON TO THE MISSING LINK OF BRIDAL READINESS,.......
THE ANNIHILATION OF JESUS OF NAZARETH.

And yes.
You ARE welcome.
You are very, very, very welcome!!

NOTES

NOTES

Chapter 4
The Opinions of Man

"The opinions of man are a <u>stench</u> in my nostrils."

While driving to speak at a small home church gathering several years back, the Lord interrupted my natural thoughts with His voice and spoke...***"The opinions of Man are a stench in my nostrils!"***

It really got my attention in a way like never before. The opinions of man are tainted with the curse of the fallen mind. And all things cursed are a stench in His nostrils.

The opinions of Man also influence us, and when we speak opinions, they influence others.

We live in a world of abiding to the opinions of influencers or influencing others with our opinions. The Mind of Christ is in total opposition to opinions, and being influenced, and being the influencer. **The only thing we are to be influenced by, is the thing we are to be annihilated by, which is the Life of Christ, which is the Mind of Christ.**

And in the annihilation of all things to bring in the redemption of all things, Christ is not overlooking the annihilating of influencers and being an influence. Overall the body of Christ, the religious church, and even those outside of anything they call Church or that is Church, we are being influenced by deception while embracing it as trend, change, and even truth. I am convinced at the top of His annihilation is the entire paradigm of influencers and being influenced. Something he spoke years ago fits in this portion very well. He spoke and said, ***"deception has become so embraced, truth is now the new deception."***

With all the above stated, these pages are NOT my opinions compiled into pages of opinions.

HOWEVER.......there is a greater chance than not, the reader WILL BE OFFENDED because the truths contained OFFEND

THE NATURAL MIND. THEY OFFEND THE FALLEN AND CURSED MIND OF MAN.

Hence the knee jerk reaction to the words shared are of the natural mind and labeled....'a stinking opinion.'

These writings have been heard in the internal and LIVED in the external. No opinions here. No stench in God's nostrils.

Know now even before reading deeper, the fallen and cursed mind of man WE ALL INHERITED WITH THE FALL OF MAN, will be offended in order to annihilate, by the truth of Christ, what MUST be removed.

The offenses are PURPOSEFUL. With the sovereign purpose to annihilate the cursed and fallen mind of man.

Embrace now as you read, the powerful truth that each of His Bride has inherited the mind of Christ. **His original intention from the foundations of the Earth has been for His Bride to possess, live through, live from, and thrive from the mind of Christ, which IS REDEMPTION!!** And it is for you, His Bride! Yet the Mind of Christ is currently hidden and buried under the muck of the highly religious, opinionated, cursed and fallen mind of man we inherited from the fall of mankind.

It is time to exchange the cursed mind we inherited from the fall, for the Mind of Christ we inherited from HIM!!

The attitude to take from here forward should be "Lord, offend me!!!!"

FOR EACH AND EVERY OFFENSE IS ANNIHILATING THE CURSED MIND AND REPLACING IT WITH THE MIND OF CHRIST!!!

NOTES

NOTES

Chapter 5
The Blind Date

"You are about to see <u>My</u> love do more than you ever thought My power would do."

I believe it is very important we begin this writing by discussing why this book has the title of, ...,

'THE BLIND DATE
The Missing Link of Bridal Readiness'

The first aspect of the blind date has already been inserted a few times in the prior four chapters, but I am going to lay it out plain and simple right here so it is not overlooked or misunderstood.

If we fully get the POINT now of what the missing link is, as we continue to read we will also fully get the TRUTH of what the missing link is and why it is absolutely mandatory for the full readiness of His Bride.

The blind date is the complete annihilation of Jesus of Nazareth. Coupled with the Life of the truth of who Christ the King of Redemption is. They are not one and the same. Although Jesus is the same yesterday, today and forever, the difference is, we are getting to know a Jesus we have never known. The forever part. The identity of Him yet to be revealed. Not just the identity or title, but the ways, words, actions, assignment, purpose, of Jesus of Nazareth annihilated unto Christ the King of Redemption. THE VASTNESS OF WHO HE IS.

This is vitally important because the Lord and Savior: Christ the King of Redemption, will not be recognized if we do not allow HIM to annihilate HIMSELF now. The annihilation of Jesus of Nazareth is so complete, thorough, scathing, and shocking, it does not leave Jesus of Nazareth in the dust. It completely annihilates even the dust.

The Life of Christ growing in our internal is the same Life of Christ, the King of Redemption, and it completely annihilates Jesus of Nazareth. To annihilate is to completely obliterate. To annihilate is total destruction without a trace of evidence of what was there before. In the process of this annihilation, the remaining self holding us back from being a completely ready bride is also annihilated, and we find ourselves a bride totally made ready.

The annihilation of Jesus of Nazareth cannot take place as fully as this book will share with you without ALL remaining self being fully surrendered and annihilated along the way. **Hence, on the blind date of getting to know Christ the King of REDMEPTION, combined with the annihilation of Jesus of Nazareth, we have the missing link that is mandatory for the TOTAL READINESS OF HIS BRIDE.**

'The Missing Link of The Blind Date', is actually a three part sovereign move.

❶ **Jesus of Nazareth is annihilated.**
❷ **Christ, the King of Redemption comes forth with His Life in our internal as the blind date of a Christ we have never known.**
❸ **And in the process, all remaining self holding on to what He is annihilating is completely removed.**

Self is removed because Jesus of Nazareth cannot be annihilated with self standing strong.

And Christ, the King of Redemption cannot come forth without self dying and stepping completely out of the way.

With the outcome being THE BRIDE MADE READY!

Let's begin with emphasizing the powerful truth that God is making a sovereign move. He is a sovereign God. He is currently and actively in a very steady cadence of the sovereign move of Redemption. Sovereignty is when God is in full control. When

God is not actively making a sovereign move, there is nothing we can do to initiate a sovereign move. However, when He is indeed actively going forward in a sovereign move, there is nothing we can do to stop it.

It is important to note we can disqualify ourself from His sovereign move by not staying in pace/cadence with Him in regard to WHAT He is doing, and the speed in which He is doing it.

THE BLIND DATE is what I am calling this sovereign move He is currently and very actively making and which takes place in the internal of His chosen vessels. We must walk each step with Him internally as CARRIERS of Christ and not simply walk following Him, or even walk with Him along our side.

THE BLIND DATE IS DESIGNED AND RESERVED FOR HIS VESSELS, WHO ARE HIS CARRIERS, NOT HIS FOLLOWERS.

By the time we are invited into His sovereign blind date, we have progressed from being in the christian club of hanging out with other Christians. We have advanced from Christianity being what we do, into who we are. Also, we would have already advanced beyond being a follower of Christ. Vessels of Christ are not Christians, and they are not followers of Christ. They are carriers of Christ who carry the Life of Christ in their internal.

One who carries the Life of Christ in their internal being is a vessel of Christ, carrying the very Life of Christ grown from the seed of Christ planted in them at salvation. When we are carriers, we are no longer followers.

I will continue by sharing in 2017 and 2018, He begin speaking to me of HIS annihilations of HIMSELF. The first time He used that word of annihilation with me was in July 2017 when he said ***"I am not coming to shift the paradigm, I am coming to annihilate the paradigm."***

A paradigm is the way we think, process, and do things. But He was speaking of Himself, therefore speaking that He was coming to annihilate the way we think, process, and do things of Him.

As He was speaking, He said ***"you are about to see My love do more than you ever thought My power would do".*** As He spoke, He was making it very clear He was coming to annihilate the paradigm of who we think, process, and believe Him to be, hence, coming to annihilate Himself. This would be done by releasing a love we had never experienced before, and it would be a love that would do more than we ever thought His power would do!

As time went on and 2017 turned into 2018, I began teaching and sharing by referring to this as the hidden manna for He is the hidden manna, and I began speaking of his Ruach Life Breath voice that would change, create, and rearrange things. I began teaching and sharing of how He was coming in a new way to present Himself to us.

At one gathering, I had been speaking and sharing on the coming annihilation, and when the meeting was over we were all visiting. For the first time that I was aware, He spoke to me internally rather than what I would typically refer to as speaking in my ear.

But I tangibly felt Him speak in my internal space of the belly area. When I shared with the people what He spoke, I included sharing with them that it was actually BREATHS OF HIS LIFE that communicated to me. I shared it was not the spoken word I typically heard in what I would call my ear, but it was Living Breaths of His Life that communicated to me.

And the message was...

"What I desire above all else is that you lay aside ALL OLD WAYS of me."

That was a different way of saying that He was coming to annihilate the paradigm of Himself. But the same message!

When He spoke the word of annihilation, I heard it via words in my ear.

But several months later, when He spoke internally, I heard it through Breaths of Life internally, and knew we were now onto something. A complete change of time. An annihilation of what we had always known OF HIM.

BECAUSE WHEN HE CHANGED THE WAY HE WAS SPEAKING TO ME, I KNEW HE WAS ALSO CHANGING WHAT HE WAS ABOUT TO SAY OF HIMSELF.

From that moment forward, He began to speak only of Himself, but not Jesus of Nazareth. He began to speak of the coming Bridegroom with the agenda of having His Bride as Christ, the King of Redemption.

THOSE WERE THE FIRST TWO ANNIHILATIONS. THE ANNIHILATION OF HOW HE SPOKE TO ME. AND THE ANNIHILATION FROM SPEAKING OF JESUS OF NAZARETH TO CHRIST THE COMING KING OF REDEMPTION. From the ear to the internal, and from words of Jesus to BREATHS OF LIFE OF THE COMING CHRIST.

Over the course of time the sharings, teachings, messages and writings were all built from the matrix of the annihilation of Himself and the taking over of His life, including His internal voice of Life Breaths, and including the location of which He was now speaking, which was the internal.

Then on February 4, 2022 He walked up to my bedside not long after I laid down one evening and spoke a very powerful message... He said.....

"I am about to make the move. NO ONE is yet aware of."

Catch that....

- **The move.**
- **<u>NO ONE.</u>**
- **Is YET aware of.**

I wanted more and I asked for more, but He was silent. Those words were also internal through His Life because He had been speaking to me ever since the above 2018 reference with His internal Life voice.

As I laid there waiting for more, I spoke to Him and said, "Lord, I know you are about to draw a dividing line between light and darkness".

He did not speak anymore that evening, but the next day, which was one of our group gatherings, I shared what He had spoken and we discussed it. Over the next few weeks, He made it very clear. **The move He was announcing, which is the move He is currently making, is the move of redemption to His original intention. His original intention when creating the Earth and everything in it and mankind.** I will share more of His original intention in another chapter.

The bedside announcement with His Life Breath voice in my internal was that He was about to make the move back to His original intention, which no one was yet aware of, of the pure and unadulterated MIND OF CHRIST!!!!

I knew this move NO ONE was yet aware of would include truly embracing, and not just being aware of Christ, the King of Redemption. As well as truly embracing the annihilation of Jesus of Nazareth. **I somehow knew the annihilation of Jesus and the introduction of Christ, the King of Redemption would ride tandem with the original intention of the pure mind of Christ *"No one was yet aware of."*** By His Life in my internal, I knew Christ the King of Redemption is the true Mind of Christ He was and currently is offering His Bride who has overcome the missing link of annihilation of herself. With the main annihilation of the bride being a letting go of Jesus of Nazareth.

SO SHE CAN BE A VESSEL OF CHRIST THE KING OF REDEMPTION.
A BRIDE MADE READY!!

Since then, which will be four years this coming February 2026, there are those of us who are actively becoming more and more aware. We are no longer "not unaware". We are growing more and more aware as we allow Him to annihilate Jesus of Nazareth and move in deeper in the internal place, the Life of Christ, the King of Redemption.

At the beginning of the process of walking with Him regarding His announcement of the soon coming move no one was yet 'aware' of, we began becoming spiritually aware. We began to have internal knowings from Him regarding what He was saying. But more so what He was releasing. Meaning we became very aware because of what HIS LIFE was bringing to us.

As time went on, we begin to become experientially aware. Encountering His Life internal with His internal voice of life, noticing changes with the increase of the Mind of Christ and less of the fallen mind of man. This process still continues and has increased. We have not arrived, but He has brought us from being not aware to becoming more and more aware in enlightenment and now into awareness through experience.

Therefore, it's no longer accurate to say No one is YET aware of. Because there are those of us becoming very aware. In the becoming aware, some of us are already experiencing the tangibility of the beginning of the exchange of the fallen mind for the original intention Mind of Christ. The full completion of the Mind of Christ will be when Christ the King of Redemption, calls His ready Bride to Himself, so that she herself can be completely annihilated and come back as the vessel of Christ, the King of Redemption.

So we began teaching, sharing, and discussing redemption into His original intention.

NOW REGARDING THE BLIND DATE....

Then, following February 2022, a few months later in November 2022, I was cleaning my kitchen and became very aware of His presence. He interrupted what I was doing by speaking again in the internal with His Life Breath voice and spoke to me and said words that I still find as exciting as I did when he spoke them. He spoke to me...

"I am about to take you on a blind date!"

The Life Breath voice internally was spoken with great excitement that I continually feel as well as hear, and I literally and loudly squealed with excitement!

Not long after that, in early 2023, He spoke to me and asked, ***"Are you ready to exchange revelations of Me for manifestations of My Life?"*** And I said, "Of course"! Knowing He meant manifestations of His Life and of this blind date.

As we know, a blind date means we are about to date someone we do NOT know, someone we have NEVER met, someone we know NOTHING about. A BLIND DATE REPLACES ANY OTHER DATE WE HAVE BEEN ON.

- **THE BLIND DATE IS THE NEW GUY!**
- **AND HE IS THE ONE WHO ANNOUNCED IT AND INVITED ME TO WHAT HE CALLED A BLIND DATE!**

THE BLIND DATE IS THE MISSING LINK! We are not a bride made ready until we go on this blind date with Him, let Him annihilate Jesus of Nazareth, and not only introduce us to Christ, the King of Redemption, but also move in our internal and take over our fallen minds.

THE MOVING IN OF CHRIST THE KING OF REDEMPTION TAKES OVER OUR FALLEN MINDS BECAUSE HIS MOVING IN IS THE MOVING IN OF THE MIND OF CHRIST.

Come Lord, Come!!!

What Christ was inviting us all into is to spend the rest of our lives with Him, getting to know the Christ of Redemption whom we have never known. It was an invitation to get to know the vastness of Christ we have never known, hence a BLIND DATE!

We have been on that blind date ever since! As He has revealed and manifested aspects of the vastness of Himself we have never known. And in doing so, He is annihilating the history of Jesus of Nazareth who we have known. We are getting to know CHRIST THE KING OF REDEMPTION!

We have been on this blind date four years now and it is getting better and better as the MIND OF CHRIST kicks out the fallen and cursed mind of man we inherited from the fall. We are now stepping into LIVING FROM THE MIND OF CHRIST!!!

The rest of these writings are comprised of short chapters that will begin to take you on your own blind date with Him! As you read them, your internal will be activated to go deeper in Him. To get to know the Christ of Redemption, we have never known.

REDEMPTION OF THE FALLEN AND CURSED MIND TO THE PERFECT MIND OF CHRIST.

You will also learn what the mind of Christ truly is.

I started out by saying when He first invited me on this blind date that everything He has taught us since then which has been three years of revelations turning into manifestations, and thus far three years of getting to know the vastness of Christ, and thus far three years of Him bringing into our internal, ways of Him we have never known, that we ARE on the blind date.

The blind date actually begins when we are redeemed, and we come forth as the redeemed of the Lord, HIS READY BRIDE FROM THE THRONE, who have the 'say so' of Psalms 107. As you continue to read, you will understand The Christ of Redemption, and what is coming for His fully surrendered vessels who will be vessels of redemption!

THOSE REDEEMED TO HIS ORIGINAL INTENTION OF A LOVE WHICH WILL DO MORE THAN WE EVER THOUGHT HIS POWER WOULD DO!!

THE TRUE BLIND DATE BEGINS WHEN HE CALLS HIS READY BRIDE TO THE THRONE AND INFUSES US WITH HIMSELF, CHRIST THE KING OF REDEMPTION, AND SENDS US BACK WITH THE FULL MIND OF CHRIST TO RULE AND REIGN WITH HIM!!

In one of the prior chapters, I referred to "utterances of him", where He spoke words of prophecy of HIMSELF. In one of those utterances He spoke...... ***"In the infusion there will be a re-infusion and you will not even recognize each other."*** The infusion is the infusion of the Mind of Christ. The re-infusion is the infusion of who He created us to be in the foundations of the Earth. His original intention for us! That is an EXCITING AND POWERFUL BLIND DATE WITH THE CHRIST OF REDEMPTION!!

We can summarize the powerful truth in this one chapter with something He spoke to me in May 2023. I was praying about a potential upcoming decision and rather than giving me the answer He spoke, yet again in the internal dwelling place of His Life and said,

"I am no longer moving into your life, I AM MOVING YOU INTO MY LIFE."

And that is exactly what the blind date with the Christ of Redemption is all about. **It's ALL about HIM, His Life, moving US into HIS Life!!**

NOTES

Chapter 6
The Missing Link

God is working with a <u>corporate</u> bride.

God is working with a corporate bride. We should know by now this is not about one individual bride being ready. This is about the readiness of a corporate bride. But what is the missing link as to why corporately we are still not yet ready?

In chapter 5, it was laid out very clearly as to what the missing link actually is. Regarding the annihilation of Jesus of Nazareth, the introduction and blind date with the Life of Christ the King of Redemption, and in the process, the complete death to self.

In this chapter, we will begin to take a look at how the missing link actually plays out and takes place in our internal. We will also be discussing a deeper aspect of the missing link not yet addressed. The aspect of 'self will' connected to the annihilation of Him.

The main key of how this plays out and takes place is that while we must be surrendered from the very beginning, or He cannot annihilate Himself nor bring in the Life of Christ the King of Redemption, we must also be open, willing, cooperative, and completely surrendered to this missing link. It is completely annihilating of all remaining self will. In particular the remaining self not willing to let go of Jesus of Nazareth.

It is vital we know the beautiful truth that death to self is not only about our personal lives although of course we should not be selfish brides. Death to self is ultimately about our self connected to Jesus of Nazareth regarding whether we cooperate with HIM and let HIM annihilate who we have truly always known Him to be that got us this far. None of us would be this far along or this close to REDMEPTION if it were not for Jesus of Nazareth.

The bride got stuck. In the death to self process regarding the death of our personal lives, we did a really good job of letting God deal with self focus and just raw nasty selfishness. But when that was complete, and we and those around us could see a difference regarding self focus and selfishness versus placing others before ourselves, we got stuck and stopped in the track of readiness. The missing link goes deeper into the internal of self and addresses self will, opinions, etc., connected to HIM.

Nothing in these writings is about dogging out Jesus of Nazareth who we have walked with, depended on and fallen in love with our entire lives. The missing link is about the deeper annihilation so self can be open, receptive, willing, and totally surrendered to not only letting go of walking hand in hand with Jesus of Nazareth, but knowing and allowing Christ the King of Redemption to annihilate Jesus of Nazareth to where there is no longer even any dust of Him remaining.

WE HAVE TO LET GO OF OUR PERSONAL AND CORPORATE HISTORY OF LOVING AND WALKING WITH JESUS OF NAZARETH WHO GOT US THIS FAR.

That is a lot of death to self will, self preference, self opinion, self grip, self religion, and so much of self that is not connected to selfish desires, wants, wishes, dreams, or even personal control of our personal lives. Including possessions, dynamics of how we live and dreams of the future.

Those things will also be annihilated. But the reason we still are not ready is because the death to self He is after, He is responding to, and He is truly getting a bride ready with, is the death of self will connected to HIMSELF.

I am going to share with you what he has shown me. In this section of the writings I will be referring to...

- **Redemption**
- **Annihilation**
- **Cadence**
- **Travail**

Following this section of the writings regarding the missing link, there will be a section regarding those above four topics of truth through which He is getting us ready.

I believe this writing is a good prerequisite to those four topics so let's begin...

The Lord has made it very clear redemption is the dawn of a new day OF HIM. It is an era OF HIM that has never been seen or lived before. It is a new expression OF HIM. This includes individual oneness that leads us into corporate readiness, and corporate oneness. In this process of oneness and readiness, we become untethered from this world and things of this world. BUT MAINLY WE BECOME UNTETHERED FROM WHO HE HAS ALWAYS BEEN.

Throughout the process, He is building governmental authority in us, and looking for the evidence of that governmental authority through us. He is referring to His Bosom as His internal location where redemption completely unfolds and we arrive completely planted in His Bosom by walking with Him breath by breath. **Walking has a specific cadence, and the cadence is inhaling and exhaling with Him.** Throughout the process of this cadence with Him, He is in the process of individual annihilations of self that bring us into a corporate ready bride.

As stated, the missing link is total annihilation of JESUS OF NAZARETH. He is doing this. I am only sharing with you about what He is doing. He is annihilating everything we have known of Him, how He operates, things He once said,

and His modes of operation. You are about to read where the missing link of annihilation has two aspects to it but these two aspects comprise the one missing link that is holding us back from complete readiness.

The missing link actually has three separate components. And within those components, annihilation has two aspects.

❶ There must be the annihilation of self WILL so complete, our total existence is surrendered unto Him and into HIM for the outcome to be that we exist in Him and through Him. Our existence becomes HIS existence. His existence becomes our existence. This is the annihilation of our fallen and cursed minds connected to who we have always known Him to be.

We are not talking about being a devoted follower of Christ, who loves Him and honors Him and serves Him. Because those are all things we already do. We are talking about being fully surrendered with the existence of our fallen minds annihilated so the existence of Christ, the King of Redemption can fill our vessel. Hence going forth victoriously to a lost and dying world.

We are talking about the true Mind of Christ with the unadulterated knowings of Christ being the force within us through which we walk in the governmental authority of Heaven. The true Mind of Christ annihilates the fallen mind of man via the government of Heaven and we become carriers of the government of Heaven.

We are talking about a level of annihilation OF SELF WILL, where we no longer even attempt to understand from the fallen mind, but we live and breathe through the knowings of the Mind of Christ.

It is a great exchange!

Annihilation takes place through cadence which you will read of later, and it takes place through travail, but ultimately it takes place by us allowing HIM to destroy every single thing we think we know of Him or we are confident we know of Him. This annihilation of what we know is because the Christ of REDMEPTION is not Jesus of Nazareth. And this all takes place with the fallen mind replaced by the Mind of Christ.

❷ The second part of the missing link is that we have got to let go of Jesus of Nazareth. This aspect is entangled within the annihilation of self will, because as we allow the annihilation of self will, which is annihilation of the fallen mind, we are then able to embrace the annihilation of Jesus of Nazareth. They are two separate parts of annihilation, but they are tightly woven together.

There must be a total annihilation of Jesus of Nazareth in order to properly and fully embrace Christ the King of Redemption. This takes place simultaneously with a total annihilation of self, and the total surrender of our existence. The two annihilations are the missing link. Although they are two separate annihilations, they go together and are woven together so tightly I am calling it THE missing link as in one missing link. **With the link that is missing comprising of self annihilation, and Jesus of Nazareth annihilation, which as prior stated brings in the third component of the missing link which is the internal invasion of the life of Christ, the King of Redemption.**

❸ The internal invasion of the Life of Christ the King of Redemption is not an annihilation. However, Christ the King of Redemption certainly does bring annihilations with Him as He comes!!! **It is the third component of the missing**

link that can now come forth once the two annihilations take place. The annihilation of self-will, combined with the annihilation of Jesus of Nazareth, paving the way for the internal invasion of the Life of Christ, the King of Redemption are the three elements of THE MISSING LINK!

Ultimately, the missing link is the fullness of the image from which we were created. In Genesis, we are told God said, **"let us make man in OUR IMAGE, after OUR likeness."** OUR IMAGE IS THE IMAGE OF THE FATHER, THE SON, AND THE HOLY SPIRIT. ALL 3 expressions of the ONENESS OF GOD.

We know the Father, the Son, and the Holy Spirit are ONE, expressed in three parts of oneness. And even though Jesus of Nazareth was fully God and fully man, without any compromise of God, redemption is the full indwelling of the image spoken of regarding man being created in OUR IMAGE.

Christ the King of Redemption, expressing the Father, the Son, and the Holy Spirit, with OUR image, for the first time truly becoming what we were created in the foundations of the Earth to be.....VESSELS OF OUR IMAGE.

Vessels of the full essence of the Trinity. No longer a man, Jesus of Nazareth, to live AMONG us. But pure and complete Divine Trinity to live WITHIN us.

As annihilation of Jesus of Nazareth truly comes forth, the fallen mind and what we thought we knew of Him is simultaneously annihilated. A blind date, indeed!!

If you are offended, that's OK because offense precedes breakthrough. Breakthrough never comes unless it is preceded by offense. When we look up the actual definition of the word breakthrough, we find that it follows an

offensive thrust. This portion of the writings is to offensively thrust you into the truth of the missing link of the bridal readiness. Annihilating self and annihilating Jesus of Nazareth. What is NOT OK and will keep us a bride not ready is remaining in the offense and not allowing it to transition into the breakthrough.

Keep reading.

NOTES

Chapter 7
What Actually Is Redemption?

"I <u>Am</u> The Third Day."

This chapter is going to begin with some beautiful things His Life breath has breathed internally and spoken. Then we are going to shift into some more specific descriptions and understandings of redemption. The understandings of redemption shared in this chapter are understandings from the Mind of Christ. I am not referring to understandings from the fallen cursed mind of man. As we grow and increase in the Mind of Christ, the understandings of intelligence from the fallen mind of man fall to the wayside, and the knowings from the Mind of Christ come forward. As those knowings mature from the Mind of Christ, they transition into redeemed understandings of the knowings of the perfected and divine Mind of Christ.

First of all redemption is the true reality of being born again Nicodemus discussed with Christ. Redemption is when the mature bride is born again through the womb of the dawn of the new day spoken of in Psalm 110. Being born again is not a prayer, a raising of the hand, a decision, or a walking down an aisle to deepen our salvation. Being born again is specifically and intentionally sovereign by the will of God. Being born again begins to take place spiritually and sovereignly now on this side of full redemption in the internal of the bride. It is all internal. Nothing about being born again is external. **Being born again is when the 'seed of salvation' matures into the Life of Christ that comes with an internal life breath voice, and with manifestations of the Mind of Christ.**

The full truth, or the full manifestation of being born again takes place when He calls us to Himself and sends us through the spiritual womb to come forth as the Manifested sons of God, the Manchild, the Redeemed of the Lord who have the say so. Redemption for the current mature bride will be when Christ calls her to His Bosom/throne and dresses her in His Holy Array of His DNA and sends her back to the Earth to rule the nations with a rod of iron.

Furthermore, HE is redemption. Christ, the King of Redemption IS redemption. The Christ referred to in this book is the manifestation of redemption and redemption is Christ the King. They are one. They are the same, one in and of the same.

Redemption comes in the third day of the sovereign time of God. Christ spoke a couple years ago internally and said... ***"I AM the Third Day."*** Sharing internally that HE IS redemption and HE IS the third day. Furthermore, redemption is the millennial reign. That rocks our theology. Because the Mind of Christ rocks and destroys ALL our theology. The Mind of Christ rocks self will to utter annihilation. The Mind of Christ rocks religion and destroys it. The Mind of Christ rocks theology.

The only readiness Christ the King of Redemption is waiting on before He comes for His bride is the internal readiness of every aspect of annihilation we are discussing in this book. He is not waiting on any type of formula, fulfillment of history, level of darkness, religious rhetoric, misconstrued eschatology, or anything else we could label or reason with our fallen mind as to why He has not yet returned for His Bride.

He is waiting for one thing and that one thing is for the missing link of the blind date of the annihilations to get her ready. When this happens, it is the millennial reign because when this happens, the full governmental authority of Heaven enters His Bride, and the millennial reign is the expression on Earth of that full governmental authority of Heaven in the Earth.

- ➲ **HE IS redemption.**
- ➲ **HE IS the third day.**
- ➲ **HE IS the millennial reign.**

Redemption is Christ, is the Mind of Christ, is the third day, is the millennial reign, is the governmental authority of Heaven, is divine order, is the seven fold spirits of God.

It's all HIM! AND ITS ALL REDEMPTION!

In May 2025, I woke three times during the night with the internal Life breath, voice speaking the following phrase each time...

"I do not honor fables, I do not honor fables, I do not honor fables!! THE BLIND LEADING THE BLIND!!!"

It was very serious and sober. I laid awake quite a bit and leaned into His internal voice until I had knowing from the Mind of Christ that developed into understandings that what He was saying to me then and what I am sharing with you now is a serious warning regarding the annihilation of Jesus of Nazareth. Ultimately what He was releasing in my internal is that as redemption comes forth, which is Christ the King of Redemption which completely annihilates Jesus of Nazareth,... at that point Jesus of Nazareth, according to Christ the King of Redemption, not according to me, but according to Christ the King of Redemption, Jesus of Nazareth is a fable.

AND THOSE NOT ANNIHILATED LEADING OTHERS ALSO NOT ANNIHILATED ARE THE BLIND LEADING THE BLIND.

A fable is a myth and a lie. He is being so clear, concrete, strong, and firm regarding the annihilation of Jesus of Nazareth that He is revealing in the internal that ....

Christ the King of Redemption has full authority and final say so over Jesus of Nazareth, being a fable, a myth, a lie!!

WHOAH!!

This is the case because of the full annihilation. Annihilation is to totally obliterate. Nothing remains. Not even dust. And for Jesus of Nazareth to be brought up and resurfaced and continued to be preached or taught when redemption is fully manifest, Christ the King is saying HE won't even recognize it. HE will not honor it. HE will not participate in it. And HIS description is a fable, a myth, a lie.

Talk about offense!

- **Those who have been on this blind date for approximately four years now.**
- **Those who have been allowing Christ the King to offend them by removing Jesus of Nazareth.**
- **Those who are already in the process of allowing Christ the King to annihilate all self will connected to Jesus of Nazareth.**
- **Those who are already allowing Christ of Redemption to replace their fallen and cursed mind with the Mind of Christ.**
- **THOSE are the bride who already understand that Christ the King of Redemption annihilates Jesus of Nazareth, and at that point, it's a fable. A lie. A myth.**

This can only be grasped through the Mind of Christ. It cannot be grasped by reading a book or a printed page. It can only be grasped through the redeemed Mind of Christ already forming in the internal of some, therefore making it very possible for the rest of us to go on this BLIND DATE with Christ the King of REDMEPTION and embrace the MISSING LINK that Jesus of Nazareth is now annihilated. Gone. Cant be found.

Anyone reading this type of book knows that when Jesus Christ died and was resurrected from the dead, He died for our redemption from sin. **The redemption being spoken of in this book is redemption back to His original intention in the foundations of the Earth before the creation of the Earth.** His original intention that mankind possess and live through the complete mind of Christ.

THE "READY BRIDE" LIVES AND OPERATES THROUGH THE MIND OF CHRIST WHICH IS WHY WE ARE STILL NOT READY.

Earlier in this book, it was stated that He came to me on February 4, 2022 and said... ***"I am about to make the move NO ONE is yet aware of."***

I have already shared this move is the move back to the original intention of the Mind of Christ. Which is redemption!

No one has yet lived with the full and complete Mind of Christ replacing the fallen and cursed mind of man we all inherited in the fall of mankind that took place in the garden with Adam and Eve. Again, the redemption spoken of in this book is the redemption back to His original intention that we operate fully in the Mind of Christ.

The redemption He is already actively in the process of taking us back to is HIS original intention, not only of the MIND of Christ, but also the oneness of marriage where the man and woman are one with Christ, therefore a complete unity of three consisting of the husband, the wife, and Christ. A oneness among all three. Also, the redemption He is already actively taking us into is where each individual person, man, woman, boy, or girl is redeemed into the Mind of Christ. Redemption places each individual and each family in full divine order of Christ as the head. Each and every INDIVIDUAL person WHO IS CHOSEN BY HIM TO BE REDEEMED TO THE MIND OF CHRIST will have the headship of the full governmental authority of Christ in their internal. NO MORE FALLEN MIND.

EACH AND EVERY REDEEMED VESSEL WILL HAVE THE FULL AUTHORITY OF HEAVEN.

The Lord asked me a few years ago in this process, ***"What is the strategy of Heaven?"*** **The answer is that the strategy**

of Heaven is divine order. With divine order being where Christ is the supreme head of the governmental authority of Heaven in each individual. That is divine order! AND THAT IS THE STRATEGY OF HEAVEN.

Divine order is Heaven's strategy of how His chosen vessels will rule and reign with HIM! And redemption is how He is taking us back to that divine order of each individual who is redeemed possessing the full governmental authority of Heaven through the complete and perfect Mind of Christ.

In redemption Christ the King of Redemption is taking us back to, each individual person will be in divine order of Christ, the King of Redemption as the head of that individual person. Each member of a marriage and each member of a family will all be redeemed back to His original intention of Christ being the head with full governmental authority of Heaven over that individual. When a marriage comes together, this will be true oneness of the husband being in oneness fully redeemed back to the divine order of Heaven where Christ is his head and the exact same will be true for the wife. And the exact same will be true for the children.

Meaning, the redemption Christ the King of Redemption is taking us back to is where each individual person in the marriage or family is standing in the divine order with Christ as the head. And when individuals come together for a marriage or family, everyone is in divine order of Christ as the head. And this is the strategy of Heaven!

The governmental authority of Heaven is the Mind of Christ and the Mind of Christ is the governmental authority of Heaven.

The governmental authority of Heaven is the sevenfold spirits of God and the sevenfold spirits of God are the governmental authority of Heaven, and they are the Mind of Christ.

Therefore, redemption is the Mind of Christ, is the governmental authority of Heaven, is the sevenfold spirits of God, is divine order, is redemption!

Christ, the King of Redemption is redeeming us back to individual vessels with the originally intended Mind of Christ, carrying the full governmental authority of Heaven of the sevenfold spirits of God. Positioning each of His chosen bride of all ages into the strategy of Heaven which is divine order!

Ultimately, redemption is when we humble ourselves before Almighty God, and allow Him to annihilate our self will over the annihilation of Jesus of Nazareth. As Jesus of Nazareth is removed from our self will, our belief systems, the religion we hold onto without even realizing, Christ the King of Redemption steps into our internal place. He talks to us internally with His Life Breath and redemption begins to take place.

The more we allow Christ the King of Redemption to remove self will regarding Jesus of Nazareth, the more internal redemption takes place. With each annihilation, we allow Him to do in our internal self will, His Life INCREASES until full redemption takes place for the corporate ready bride.

The ultimate completion of redemption will manifest based on Revelation 12 when He calls His bride to Him and infuses her with HIS DNA. The manchild who will rule the nations with a rod of iron is the expression of the redeemed.

The blind date, the missing link to bridal readiness, comes to full and complete readiness when Christ the King of Redemption sees annihilated self will, and the internal of the vessel being possessed and increasing with the Life of Christ, the King of Redemption. When He sees that corporately His chosen bride has progressed internally with the seed of salvation, growing and maturing in the Life of Christ the King of Redemption, He will see the degree of readiness He is looking for to bring us to His Bosom, His throne, and complete the redemption by infusing us with HIS DNA. His Life. His governmental authority. The Mind of Christ. Divine order. The sevenfold Spirit of God. And His manchild will be sent back to the Earth to indeed rule and reign the nations.

- **Redemption is the dawn of the new day.** It is the new era that has never been seen before, but it's already opening up for those who have been walking with Him internally in this process of redemption.
- **Redemption produces the divine oneness** of each individual and Christ the King of Redemption.
- **Redemption untethers us from this world,** things of this world, the fallen and cursed mind of man, and infuses us with the Mind of Christ.

Currently, we are not in divine order, but we will be in HIS divine order when full redemption takes place. Nothing in our current existence is in divine order, except for the internal of those who are already in the process of this blind date with Him and steps away from full redemption. Anything we expect to be the same once redemption fully manifest is deception. Our lives will not be the same or even recognized as the same. We will be seen as HIM. We will be seen as HIS vessels. HE will be our identity. HE will be our light. HE will be our authority. We will have HIS mind. The knowings of Christ the King of Redemption will override the understanding of the fallen and cursed mind.

AND PRAISE HIM FOR THAT!!! And He will have His Bride whom He has longed to be with in the truth of the vastness of who He is.

Come Lord, Come!!!

NOTES

NOTES

Chapter 8
His Gifts of Annihilation, Cadence, and Travail

"For the beauty for ashes are My Priest in the order of Melchizedek"

The three powerful truths of annihilation, cadence and travail work together in this process of redemption. With each being their own separate aspect of the redemption process, yet they are intricately connected and operate with each other and off of each other. Much has already been said about annihilation, but we're going to take a look at annihilation, cadence, and travail to see how they work together, and how they carry us all the way to full redemption of the Mind of Christ.

There is a likely chance this chapter will seem heavy and complicated. **I encourage each of us to press on because as you continue to read not only this chapter, but the remaining chapters of this book it is all going to come together by way of His Life breathing the knowings of the Mind of Christ in our internal. Just remain open and teachable to His perfect plan.**

His ANNIHILATION as we have seen is utter destruction, leaving no trace of any prior existence behind. Whether it be the annihilation of our self will or the annihilation of Jesus of Nazareth. **His CADENCE** is His heartbeat that moves His Life forward. As He moves forward, we must move forward in perfectly aligned cadence with Him. His cadence is His method of how we move with Him deeper into redemption unto the full bursting forth of redemption. **TRAVAIL**, plain and simple, is the pain of the process. It gets hard along the way, but when we keep our eyes fixed on Him and where He is taking us, the pain is as beautiful as giving birth to a baby. Because once we hold that child, we forget the pain. His travail is pain with a beautiful purpose.

Regarding annihilation, it is total destruction unto obliteration of the matter at hand. Of course, we are referring to the fallen and cursed mind of a man being completely annihilated into the Mind of Christ, along with Jesus of Nazareth being completely annihilated unto Christ the King of Redemption. **We must stay alert that everything He is doing is internal. Because the internal dwelling place of a vessel is where His Life resides.** His Life that comes forth when the seed of salvation has grown and matured into His Life with expressions of His Life. His Life lives in the internal place and does the work internally, even though sometimes the internal work produces external actions and reactions, or requires external actions and reactions.

An example would be His Life doing an internal work of annihilation which then produces a required move to another geographical area, change in a relationship, or change with our occupation, etc. **The work is always done internally, but sometimes it flows into external actions or reactions. But overall, no matter what, HE IS annihilating the INTERNAL.** We are to become the annihilated Bride who recognizes the annihilated Christ. This takes place when our natural and fallen minds are annihilated and increasing in His Life, His governmental authority, and His internal knowings. Hence it takes place internal, and of course, the annihilation is with a corporate outcome with each Bridal vessel going through the annihilation process.

Even this very moment, while writing this, He is showing me internally that He is even annihilating the corporate bride as a whole and not just individually.

He is internally showing me the outcome of the annihilation of the corporate bride is that the remnant who come forth from the corporate annihilation will come forth from the ashes of the annihilation, and the 'beauty for ashes' spoken of in Isaiah 61 are the Priest in the order of Melchizedek.

A few years back, He spoke what I have prior referred to as an utterance when He would speak prophetic utterances of

Himself and part of that utterance which was around 2020, was...

"For the beauty for ashes are my Priest in the order of Melchizedek."

But in this very moment of writing, He is showing me the ashes are the annihilation of the corporate bride. **This is very sobering because what He is in this moment revealing internally of Himself is that the corporate bride as it is this very day will be annihilated to ashes, and from the ashes will come forth the remnant who HE is calling his Priest in the order of Melchizedek.**

Although we in this process of "the move He is making" shared in these writings have known this to be true in that the ashes are His Priest, He is in this moment, revealing not just the annihilation of the individual bride, so the annihilated INDIVIDUAL bride can recognize the annihilated Christ, but He is saying the overall outcome of the annihilation corporately will be only a remnant who will believe the truths shared in this small book due to a corporate annihilation unto ashes and those of the corporate bride surviving the annihilations will be His Priest coming forth from the ashes of the corporate annihilation.

I also love He is bringing this forth in this very moment of writing because He is sharing with us that one of the most popular scriptures from His word of Isaiah 61:3.....Beauty for ashes... Which has always been translated to mean good things for our bad things, or blessings for our trials and suffering, is being annihilated into HIS TRUTH the beauty for the ashes are His priest in the order of Melchizedek. NOT PERSONAL REWARDS FOR OUR LOSSES.

This is a perfect example of the annihilated Christ, speaking with breaths of Life in the internal, the truth of who He really is, overriding the traditions of men and fallen interpretations and understandings from a fallen and cursed mind of man.

Perfect example! "Beauty for ashes" ARE HIS PRIEST COMING FORTH FROM THE ANNIHILATED CORPORATE BRIDE.

And what a mindblower it is to the fallen and cursed mind of man that HE is using annihilations of Jesus of Nazareth to corporately annihilate HIS VERY OWN BRIDE.

In the process (being mentioned above before He came internally and began speaking of the corporate annihilation of His Bride), the process of walking into redemption and waiting on the full manifestation of redemption, there is a lot of annihilation of the paradigm of the fallen logical mind taking place. So much annihilation of the logical mind of man I have often been offended by what Christ has instructed me personally to do, but in the surrender and obedience, the offense falls away and more of His Life moves in and takes over my fallen mind. Hence the annihilation of the logical and cursed mind unto the mind of Christ. Step by step. Annihilation by annihilation.

This is absolutely a work of Him and His life! This is not a work for others or us to do, or it fails completely. He does the work and we respond to what He is doing internally.

Annihilation doesn't come in one blow, but rather it is an active process that takes place with His cadence. His cadence is His forward movement of taking us into redemption. He is in a very steady, consistent, and firm cadence which is of vital importance for us to know. For if we do not stay in cadence with Him, we lag behind and risk lagging too far behind to be included in the process of bridal readiness. He is on the backside of this readiness regarding wrapping it up. If we are not in cadence, we need to get in cadence with Him and remain in cadence with Him for He is moving forward very quickly.

IF WE DO NOT MOVE FORWARD WITH HIM WE LOSE OUR POSITION IN HIM.

His cadence currently is very focused and firm and steady. As His life increases internally, we become very aware of the force of His cadence, the speed of His cadence, and the description of His cadence. THANK YOU HOLY ONE FOR YOUR FAITHFULNESS!!

The description of His cadence is also discerned internally and in regards to knowing the dynamics of the cadence. Not just the force or the forward movement of His cadence. This is where cadence ties into annihilation. When His cadence does include a change in a relationship, a change in a job, or a change in the dynamics of anything we are doing in order to be able to continue moving forward with Him, it is because He desires us to move forward with the same force and pace in which He is moving forward. Meaning that His cadence rides hand-in-hand with annihilation. As internal annihilations come forth there is always a shift in our belief system of who He is and what He is doing along with these sometimes external requirements that lineup with the annihilation and the cadence. We must not limit His cadence to external changes within our lives, nor should we limit them to the internal annihilations of what we know of Him. They play out together in many situations though sometimes His cadence is only internal and sometimes only external, but they often ride together.

His cadence is the reality of moving deeper into oneness with Him! By staying in the CADENCE OF ONENESS with Him, we arrive at the full outward manifestation of complete redemption, a full vessel of CHRIST THE KING!

Redemption is a culmination of time, not "A"time. Redemption is the culmination of time where His life in us brings us face-to-face with Him. **His current mode of operation to get us to His Bosom and His face, is His cadence!** The culmination of time is when those He is waiting on know His cadence, and corporately, as He is headed toward us, we run straight into Him!! OH HOW I LOVE THAT!

As the annihilations go deeper, and as the cadence becomes more forceful with a faster pace, this is when travail begins to become the third leg of this process. **Travail is the painful process of going deeper into the Mind of Christ and leaving more of the mind of man behind.** The travail arrives and when it does indeed require external changes in the dynamics of where we live, where we work, who we do life with, relationships, etc., etc., travail is the dynamic of the internal hardship and heartache of going deeper in oneness with Him. Oneness with Him requires the loss of things of this world and the loss of our identity. It's easy to see that annihilation comes with cadence and the cadence of the annihilations take us deeper into Him and more away from life as we have known it. When we arrive at this point, the travail begins to be a very painful and powerfully dynamic.

OH BUT WHAT A BEAUTIFUL OUTCOME NO MATTER THE PAIN! HE IS WORTHY OF IT ALL!

The beautiful three part harmony of annihilation, cadence and travail, leads us directly into the strategy of Heaven, which is divine order. When we stay focused on the outcome of redemption unto the Mind of Christ which gives us the full authority of the entire government of Heaven, there is a grace upon this harmony of moving us from fallenness into oneness.

WHAT A GREAT EXCHANGE!
FALLENNESS INTO ONENESS!

Redemption IS the Mind of Christ. Therefore, if we are to live from redemption, even now, we are living from the Mind of Christ and the more we live from the Mind of Christ, the more the fallen mind is completely annihilated and falls away. No longer existing.

As this beautiful three part harmony of annihilation, cadence and travail lead us into the beauty of His oneness, it is not uncommon to become internally frustrated toward outward situations that do not lineup with what He is doing and where His cadence is taking our internal. **The OUTWARD circumstances of our lives will often directly clash with the INTERNAL work He is bringing forth.** There was a time when He was annihilating my internal in such a fast, steady, harsh pace to keep me in cadence with Him, I was continuously repenting to Him for my internal frustrations because nothing in life was in sync with what He was doing internally. At one point when I was crying out to Him repenting over my attitude with the struggle, He spoke to me very clearly with His Life voice, and said, *"It is not your attitude, it is your position!"*

MEANING MY POSITION IN HIM WAS PRODUCING CONFLICT WITH THE INTERNAL.

Another time He said, ***"you are not frustrated outside of me, and I am not frustrated outside of you, we are in this together."*** This was the outcome of Him forming oneness between the two of us.

He was showing me the alignment of frustrations as well as the alignment of oneness with Him by telling me we were in it together. When He spoke to me that it was not my attitude, but rather it was my position, He was letting me know that I was internally adjusting to where He was taking me. It was a spiritual alignment and a spiritual adjustment. When He said it is not your attitude it is your position, the position He was speaking of is the position of deeper annihilation, therefore closer to His heart of redemption. He was speaking to me that way to let me know there was not a need for repentance, but yet to show me that internally, I was very aware of what He was doing in me. By being internally frustrated, I was in alignment with the annihilating cadence He had me in at the moment. He was approving of my awareness of what HE was doing by letting me know there was no need for repentance. He and I were in it together.

ANNIHILATION PRODUCES THE UNRECOGNIZABLE, until HIS LIFE comes internally and lines us up with HIM.

I did not recognize my irritations and frustrations were of Him until the internal awareness of the Mind of Christ gave me the knowing of what He was doing. His cadence is His mode of operation to get us to the unrecognizable and travail shows up in the process. It is painful to leave Jesus of Nazareth behind, but it is His annihilation, and it is His cadence that propels us directly into redemption. DIRECTLY INTO HIM.

What we need to truly believe and realize, tightly grasp and not let go of is that the annihilated Christ the King of Redemption is already geared up and running forward at a very steady cadence of annihilation, leaving behind Him a trail of travail in the process of the death of our self will over Jesus of Nazareth. **We must catch up. Redemption of the Mind of Christ and the second coming of Christ in His Bridal vessels is not something we are waiting on. HE IS ACTIVELY DOING IT.**

He is actively taking His most mature bride with Him in this cadence of annihilation even while they suffer great travail of the destruction of their self will directly into the bosom of redemption of the fallen and cursed mind into the redeemed Mind of Christ.

We do not have time to lag behind. We must get in cadence with Him and suffer the travail of leaving Jesus of Nazareth behind. Geared up with Him and going forward in the annihilation of self will to get the job done.

If we disagree, think too hard, lag behind, or doubt these truths, it could be a death blow to our individual readiness because He is already actively moving forward in a very steady cadence.

His cadence starts with internal knowings of what He is communicating to us. Then His cadence, as we mature, progresses into internal knowings of what He wants us to speak and decree on His behalf regarding this process of very active redemption that is already quickly unfolding. After the maturity of the internal knowings from the beginning of the mind of Christ of what He is saying, and the maturity of the internal knowings of what to decree and speak of His will, His cadence changes to what He has called the "zero tolerance"cadence.

The zero tolerance cadence is what gets us around that last lap of the race and to the final flag of winning the race of redemption.

The zero tolerance cadence is when He tells us internally either things He is requiring of us that involve ACTION, or things He is speaking of Himself which require ANNIHILATION.

Whereas cadence always came with requirements and annihilations, the degree is up with the zero tolerance cadence. The requirements get much harder and the annihilations go much deeper.

Zero tolerance means there is zero tolerance to entertain any understanding from the fallen mind. DONT FORGET THAT !! Zero tolerance cadence means we do not understand why, but we do internally know what HE wants from us. When the zero tolerance cadence begins to take place in the internal, we will have progressed enough with Him to know He is speaking to the developing Mind of Christ in our internal. When He is speaking to the developing Mind of Christ, which is the process of redemption, we are to know from the Mind of Christ what He wants and the zero tolerance is to not involve the fallen mind of understanding at all.

NOT. AT. ALL.

Plain and simple, zero tolerance means to leave the fallen mind out of the process. Don't look for understanding. The cadence is knowing exactly what HE is saying and doing. And we are to operate from the knowing of the mind of Christ and have nothing to do with a 'zero tolerance' of the fallen mind within that cadence. **When the knowings come, we are to take action without seeking understanding of who, what, when, where, why, and how.**

An example of a zero tolerance cadence means that we absolutely know, that we know, that we know what He wants of us, but we do not have understanding from the fallen mind and to 'why' He wants what He does. Zero tolerance is how He has stated He does not want us to try to understand what is coming to us from the Mind of Christ by glancing back at the fallen mind to try to get understanding. They don't mix. THE CURSED FALLEN MIND DOES NOT MIX WITH THE PERFECTED AND DIVINE MIND OF CHRIST. Therefore, when He speaks from the Mind of Christ, we are not to even glance back at the fallen mind and try to understand. We are to simply know He has spoken and do accordingly.

The zero tolerance cadence gets us all the way to the end of the race and we arrive at redemption. When He spoke to me of zero tolerance cadence and not simply cadence, He said, "*the* *zero tolerance cadence gets us all the way to the completion of redemption and it annihilates the remaining fallen mind."* This means the closer we get with Him in our internal to full redemption unto the Mind of Christ, He will require things of us internally that come with scathing shifts in our belief systems of who He is regarding Christ the King of Redemption. Along with scathing shifts in our belief system of the annihilated Jesus of Nazareth, combined with very hard obedience.

When we find ourselves at the place of zero tolerance cadence where we are operating internally and externally ONLY from the mind of Christ, that is our road marker that redemption is about to burst forth in Christ. The King of Redemption is about to call His Bride to Himself because that is the sign of complete readiness.

I will repeat that. When the corporate bride is operating in zero tolerance cadence and staying in exact pace with Him......A pace that involves scathing annihilations internally of who we believe Him to be as Christ the King of Redemption and scathing annihilations internally of Jesus of Nazareth......combined with obedience that makes no sense to the fallen mind while knowing from the Mind of Christ it is what HE wants of us....THAT is our road marker that we are a bride made ready and it is time for Him to gather His READY corporate bride TO HIMSELF! WHEW!!!! All I know to say is WHEW!!!

It gets very rocky at the end.

It is important to know the aspect that can make zero tolerance cadence so annihilating is because zero tolerance cadence more often than not totally annihilates any prior cadence. Meaning it leaves the prior cadence He brought forth in our internal to its own point of annihilation, and leaves cadence in the dust. **Not cadence altogether, but the prior cadence of**

what He clearly showed us was absolutely of Him on this road to redemption is often annihilated by the next cadence He releases. It's not just that each movement of cadence takes us farther and closer, but when we look behind, the prior cadences aren't imprinted in the sand. They no longer exist. This is where it can get challenging and why it is so widely important we grow in the Mind of Christ. Because the Mind of Christ are the sure knowings of Christ. He often annihilates the prior cadence when He releases a new cadence as a deeper process of annihilating the understanding of the fallen mind. Because HE is in a cadence of annihilations, He does not want us leaning on or depending on any cadence of the past. Just keep moving forward with HIM!

As cadence progresses, His focus shifts more to internal cadence yet not to fully eliminate external cadence. **The purpose of the internal cadence of the 'say so' of the Mind of Christ is to fully annihilate the remaining fallen mind. The internal cadence is annihilating belief systems and thought patterns of not only who He is, but now including deeper aspects of our fallen nature.** Annihilating Himself while simultaneously annihilating us individually.

The internal cadence now carries the 'say so' of the process and even the 'say so' of when He comes for His Bride because the zero tolerance cadence comes at the very end. The zero tolerance cadence is when He is wrapping things up. The zero tolerance cadence puts us on the fast track of cadence to Him and the culmination of time as we know it. The cadence where we leave the fallen mind totally out of the process. Zero tolerance of the fallen mind participating in the cadence is how we have the 'say so' of when redemption is fully manifested, the bride is made ready to completion, and He comes for His annihilated Bride who will recognize the annihilated Christ when He arrives.

The zero tolerance cadence is a zero tolerance and annihilation of...

- **Jesus of Nazareth**
- **Things of this world**
- **The remaining fallen mind refusing to let go of Jesus of Nazareth**

We are not in charge of how hard the zero tolerance cadence gets. Our participation is to respond to them and not try to figure them out for that would be exercising the fallen mind He is annihilating. We are to know they get us to redemption and stay in full galloping cadence with Him. At the end of the race, everything becomes about His zero tolerance cadence even when His current cadence annihilates the prior cadence. It becomes no longer about what He prior said to us. It becomes all about what He is currently saying to us. Everything He says to us at this point comes from the knowing internally from the Mind of Christ. If we are searching for understanding, we are exercising the fallen mind which is to be in a serious process of atrophy.

When cadence with Him has reached the zero tolerance cadence we are at the point in this process where He now has no tolerance for us tapping into understanding of the fallen mind and we find ourselves living through the internal knowings of the mind of Christ. The internal knowings from His Mind will annihilate all we once knew of Him. They will defy logic. They will remove the religion and rules of the past. The Mind of Christ is where we reside from this point forward and it takes us to the completion of redemption.

Along the way there is much travail because travail is the pain we experience the deeper we step into oneness with the Mind of Christ. Stepping into oneness with the Mind of Christ is not simply a decision we make. It is a painful process. And that process is the travail.

His annihilation, His geared up cadence, and His travail that all take us into the oneness of the Mind of Christ are His gifts to us. They are His gifts to get us from being not ready to being the corporate bride made ready.

And when we arrive, we won't even recall how hard and impossible it was with HIM DOING IT IN US. We submit. BUT HE DOES THE BEAUTIFUL WORK IN US.

ALL GLORY TO HIM!

NOTES

NOTES

Chapter 9
Kill The Frogs And Slaughter The Oxen

Everything He is doing is <u>internal</u>.

He is corporately asking us the question of, do you want to spend another night with the frogs? You most likely recognize that reference to the frogs from the context of when Moses was dealing with Pharaoh. It is a corporate question because the frogs represent captivity. The fallen mind of man He is replacing in this beautiful gift of redemption is a cursed mind. **His original intention is that we all have the full and uncompromised Mind of Christ. He is redeeming us back to his original intention of the perfected Mind of Christ.**

In the meantime we are all unknowingly choosing to spend one more night with the frogs. Regarding the Pharaoh, self life, position, power, and control were way more important to him than letting the people go to their freedom. Even the grossly large detail of choosing to hold onto the frogs one more night because if he let Moses remove the frogs, that was submission to letting the people go. His SELF WILL had not been annihilated unto Gods will.

As we continue to spend another night, and another night, and another night, and another year, and another year, and another year, with the frogs representing self, control, power, position, and captivity of the fallen mind not annihilated unto Christ the King of Redemption, then we are choosing to remain a Bride not ready. And we are missing the powerful link of annihilation. Pharaoh was not ready for annihilation. He was not even aware of annihilation because the entire truth and concept of annihilation was a direct opposition to all he represented and was holding onto.

HE is writing a storyline with us that leads to redemption and giving us beautiful road markers along the way. He has given us puzzle pieces that all go together for a message of what He's manifesting in the internal of His Bride, how close we are to the completion of readiness, and letting us lovingly know the missing link holding us back.

When He speaks, we are to connect everything to the entire storyline of redemption and not dissect or disconnect any one message from Him as to meaning a separate and single message He is speaking to us corporately. For He is speaking with connectivity. When we connect everything He is speaking regarding the annihilation of self and of Jesus of Nazareth, then when we embrace them internally, we will find ourselves a Bride made ready. It is THEN when He will fulfill His promise of returning in the internal of His bridal vessels who have been humble enough to allow Him to annihilate themselves AND Himself into, and unto perfected readiness.

Everything He is doing is internal. Sometimes the internal annihilations require external actions and reactions such as moving to a different area or changing and switching relationships we have been involved in. But overall, no matter what, He is annihilating the internal of us and all things of Him. When we are the completely annihilated Bride, we will recognize the annihilated Christ. Those words are so powerful I will repeat them...

When we are the completely annihilated Bride, we will recognize the annihilated Christ/Jesus of Nazareth, who has become Christ, the King of Redemption.

I just shared that with you because as I was traveling one day, he spoke clearly in the internal and said...

"It will only be my annihilated bride who will recognize the annihilated Christ."

That my dear corporate bride is readiness. That is our missing link. That is how we get there. AND THAT IS A WARNING! With Him saying, it will only be the annihilated bride who recognizes the annihilated Christ, He is letting us know right there, if we are not annihilated of self will of who He has been, and who

He already has become, we will not recognize Him when He is ready for us.

MAJOR WARNING!!

NOT ALLOWING HIM TO ANNIHILATE 'SELF WILL', THE FALLEN MIND OF WHO HE NO LONGER IS, WHO HE HAS BECOME, AND HOW HE IS WRAPPING THIS UP, WILL CAUSE US TO TOTALLY MISS WHO WE THOUGHT WE WERE WAITING ON.

And we will find ourselves a foolish virgin, deceptively standing in a puddle of false readiness having been counted out. No oil in our lamps. Because the oil in the lamps of the wise bride is the oil of gladness that flows from Christ, the WARRIOR King of Redemption coming to marry His Bride who originally fell in love with Jesus of Nazareth.

If we are choosing another night with the frogs, we are choosing to corporately remain not ready. He knows the quota of the corporate who must be fully annihilated and fully ready for Him to come. I invite you to be a willing part of that quota.

If we do not want to spend another night with the frogs, then we go deeper in this annihilation and in this travail. We need to know we all still have some pharaoh in our internal if we're holding onto anything of us and anything of Jesus of Nazareth which must be let go so the frogs can hop away. Letting go of every frog from the internal, so there is no longer any identified pharaoh in our internal, becomes a scathing annihilation that will bring on true travail.

He is currently getting all the pharaoh out of us and His mode of operation is annihilation. The pharaoh in our internal is anything we don't want Him to remove that is clogging up the arteries of going deeper into individual oneness and corporate oneness with Christ, the King of Redemption.

This is because He has chosen us to be vessels of HIMSELF who sets the captives free. Therefore, all frogs must croak. No pun intended.

He has also been tying this into the account where Elijah called Elisha into ministry which is found in first Kings 19. Elisha was active with his life and plowing with 12 oxen, but when he finally understood that Elijah was calling him into himself and out of his personal life, he turned and slaughtered the oxen, demonstrating walking away from his own life. **God is inviting us to simultaneously allow HIM to remove the INTERNAL frogs while WE slaughter the EXTERNAL Oxen.** This produces a deeper internal annihilation, bringing us closer to readiness and produces a deeper internal untethering of this world and the fallen and cursed mind of man we are so grossly addicted to.

When we are internally annihilated, no matter what we still possess externally, and no matter what we are still involved with and committed to externally, nothing has a hold on us, for we will be so annihilated we are totally untethered from the external. Being untethered does not mean we are not committed to people and we do not possess things. It also does not mean we no longer desire or enjoy things. Being untethered means nothing has a hold or grip on us. On the other side of that coin, we also have no grip on the internal or the expression of our lives external. Nothing grips us. And we grip nothing. BUT HIM.

Being untethered does not mean we no longer have DESIRE for commitments and possessions. It means we no longer have BONDAGE to commitments and possessions.

He wants to ask you, are you wanting to spend another

night with the frogs?

Are you willing to slaughter the ox who represent your life, your security, your provision?

He has shown the oxen mainly represent our EXTERNAL individual lives and how they look, what they are made of, and who we are connected with. While the frogs mainly represent that which still remains in the INTERNAL mindsets with both the oxen and the frogs needing the complete annihilation that propels us to readiness.

All these annihilations start internal whether they end up involving the external or not. They start internal with the negotiations of self running to Elijah and saying can I do this first, or can I do that first, or let me finish up this, or what about that, or what about this?

Then we progress into negotiating with self and going back-and-forth with self either running it by the Lord to see if He approves or disapproves. Then we find ourselves finally running back to slaughter the oxen. It is first and foremost an internal work that ends up manifesting in the external at some point. And that point is a very important and vital point of arrival. Elisha negotiated with himself internally before he was able to turn and slaughter the oxen externally.

The final removal of every frog and the final slaughtering of every oxen will fully manifest when Christ the King of Redemption makes His move of redemption when He calls His Bride to Himself and sends her back in His sovereign move of redemption. However, much slaughter of oxen and much removal of frogs is in the process NOW. And is mandatory to be a Bride made fully ready.

MUCH death to self will must take place for the missing link

of annihilation of self will, AKA the fallen and cursed mind of man, for the annihilation of Jesus of Nazareth to take place. Therefore, fulfilling and conquering the missing link of readiness that has kept us from complete readiness.

Much of these writings are in regards to the annihilation of Jesus of Nazareth unto the manifestation of Christ, the King of Redemption. I encourage you not to allow a lack of understanding from the fallen mind block you regarding that powerful truth. Just hang in there and push forward.

With annihilation of Jesus of Nazareth being the missing link to our complete readiness, we must know that annihilation means to be destroyed to no existence.

Our lives are absolutely not to look the same at all. He is looking for the internal slaughter now while we remain committed and surrendered. Letting go INTERNALLY of all external possessions, situations and commitments even when still involved.

Jesus of Nazareth must be destroyed to no existence, and this is done by annihilating us so He can annihilate Himself.

Don't forget the powerful truth that whether YOU are ready or not, HE IS COMING! SOON!! And when He comes, He's not going to be Jesus of Nazareth. NOR WAIT FOR YOU TO GET READY. He's going to be Christ the King of Redemption. His appearance, His physical appearance will not even be the same. His countenance will be nothing of the same. We are very close to that day of reckoning. If we do not let Him totally annihilate our existence/self will, opinions, and Jesus of Nazareth, no amount of readiness will have us ready to recognize someone we don't yet know. And in many cases have never even heard of.

WE MUST GET TO KNOW HIM NOW AS CHRIST THE KING OF

REDEMPTION OR WE WILL BE STANDING THERE LOOKING FOR A MAN WHO NO LONGER EXIST!!

This is why He spoke with His Life and revealed that Christ the King of Redemption will only, only, only be recognized by the annihilated bride.

And furthermore, the annihilated Christ will only, only, only come back for the annihilated bride.

And the power punch of it all is Christ will only, only, only possess, fill, reside in, and USE the annihilated bride.

He showed me two or three years ago most of even His people which, of course would be who He calls His Bride, the true people of God, the true church, His bride... Most will not recognize Him, and most will not survive the destruction of Jesus of Nazareth.

Leaving a remnant willing to allow HIM to annihilate them AND Himself.

And that my dear corporate friends is why we are not ready.

Of those of us still in the race of Bridal readiness, most of us still standing, will not make the cut and be standing in this annihilation when He arrives for those who were willing to surrender Jesus of Nazareth and the self will of the fallen and cursed mind of man holding onto the hem of His garment.

There will be a few. There will be a remnant, desperate enough to let go of the fallen and cursed mind of man we are grossly addicted to. With the strongest addiction of the bride being the addiction to Jesus of Nazareth.

HE is yelling loudly to the individual fallen and cursed minds of man with a loud cry of............

LET MY PEOPLE GO!!!!!

The missing link of readiness must come forth, so the quota of ready bride He is waiting upon in His Bosom is annihilated of self, and looking for Christ the King of Redemption having long said goodbye to Jesus of Nazareth.

If we are still holding on to even one minuscule aspect of Jesus of Nazareth, refusing to let go of what we think we know with our depraved, fallen, and cursed minds, we will never recognize or be chosen by Christ the King of Redemption.

NOTES

NOTES

Chapter 10
The Book of Life

Christ, the King of Redemption Is the Book of Life.

First and foremost, the Book of Life IS HIM. Christ, the King of Redemption IS the Book of Life, HIS LIFE. We are warned in His word to not have our names blotted out of the book of life. This is because from the foundations of the Earth, HE chose us and placed our names in the book of life, meaning He placed our names WITHIN HIMSELF.

Those who have begun the entrance walk of redemption, those who will join us on this path, and all of us who will make it completely into the bosom of redemption to the original intention of the full unadulterated Mind of Christ are those who will never experience being blotted out of His book of life. We will never encounter the grevious truth of being blotted out of HIM. This sad and sobering truth is that this blotting out, or removal, happens gradually and without most people knowing until they face eternity outside of Him.

I cannot phantom not being aware of HIM. I cannot fathom living life outside of Him. I cannot fathom missing His daily intentionally woven intervention in our lives. Oh how beautifully intentional He is!! And I cannot fathom being blotted out.

He is specifically intentional. Every word He speaks, every sound He utters, every breath He takes, every protection in which He stands, every blessing He releases, every encounter of Him, every interaction with others, every moment of every day is specifically and intentionally ordained, initiated, and watched over by Him.

HE WRITES A DAILY LOVE LETTER OVER EACH OF HIS BRIDE OF HIS BEAUTIFUL AND SPECIFIC INTENTIONS OF HIS HEART INTO HERS.

Yet the human nature which is a byproduct of the fallen and cursed mind, has a strong tendency to overlook all the above and wander aimlessly through this life without Him and without His specific intentions. Nothing is by chance, or a mistake, or happenstance. He is God, Almighty! He is Creator! He is on the throne, specifically and intentionally initiating, activating, and watching over all!

I encourage you to live this way. Knowing that He is specifically intentional. Knowing His intricate and active involvement in every aspect of your life in Him. We are not outside of Him. None of us are. None of us written in the Book of Life are outside of Him. Our names do not get blotted out when we live our lives within the engraving of our names, residing within Him.

It's a great exchange! As we abide and reside IN HIM within the engraving of our name, HE abides and resides within us. This is the best protection and insurance plan of Him, assuring our names are not blotted out.

Note: The key to not being blotted out of the Book of Life, which is Him, is to overcome. When we overcome this world and this life, we are not blotted out. **The beautiful mystery of that overcoming is, that it is only because of Him we are equipped to overcome. We ourselves cannot overcome. It is not a self work or a self victory. It is HIS LIFE IN US that causes the overcoming.** Therefore, He has not only written our names within Himself, He has equipped us with Himself to overcome and not be blotted out. Clearly, being indeed blotted out is due to a lack of His overcoming life, causing us to be removed from HIMSELF.

The beauty in all of this is that He Himself is the guarantee and the covering of the very beauty that we are written within Him. He wrote our names in the Book of Life to be guaranteed recipients and victors of His complete redemption. THIS IS BECAUSE REDEMPTION IS HIS LIFE. Then covered us with His Life to overcome and walk in that redemption. When we continually choose self will over His will, we exchange His guarantee of life for satan's guarantee of self and pride, which brings about the grievous blotting out.

I cannot fully fathom the gift of being written IN Him, and then also covered BY Him to be included WITH Him in redemption! Yet He is bringing forth from the mind of Christ, the beauty of His holiness of the Book of Life being a collection of our names written in His Life. The Mind of Christ is opening up the beauty of it all. An eternal listing of those who are receiving and will receive the redeemed gift of His Life to live in redemption on this Earth WITH HIM.

The reality of what He is revealing of Himself to us is that the book of life is the book of redemption! For HE is redemption. For redemption is HIM, His life is redemption! And His redemption is His life!

When we truly grasp that our names are internally and eternally engraved in Him, for He is redemption, and He IS the Book of Life, we should be humbly motivated to allow Him to bring forth every aspect of our Bridal readiness, according to His divine plan of annihilation of self and annihilation of Jesus of Nazareth.

Definitely a beautiful exchange!

NOTES

Chapter 11
The Ruach Life Breath of God

Redemption is the perfected restoration of GODs original intention.

When God created the Earth and everything on it and in it including mankind, He first had the knowing of His will, then He spoke His perfect will, and the words spoken created the coming forth of His will. He KNEW before he SPOKE. But when He spoke, creation came forth from the power and authority of His voice. And His will was created.

He KNEW. He SPOKE. He CREATED. And His will came forth.

He had then and still has an original intention. His original intention is the outcome of His original will, and plan. For mankind to live in perfect harmony with the Father, the Son, and the Holy Spirit. For mankind to live in perfect Harmony with each other. To live in perfect harmony with creation. His original intention included for all of mankind to be loved and to love others with the same love through which God loves us.

This original intention was put to a stop in the garden with Adam and Eve via the test of doubt with the serpent. The serpent planted doubt in Eve, not by telling her what to do, but by causing her to doubt God by asking her, ***"did God really say do not eat the fruit of this tree?"***

The seed of doubt was planted by suggesting she question God's heart within His directives, the apple was eaten, and the fall of mankind came forth. As we step into redemption, God's original intention for the perfection of mankind, creation, His love, and His will, ALL come forth and grow into the fullness of His original intention.

Redemption is the perfected restoration of Gods original intention. Redemption is Christ the King as perfect restoration of God's original intention via the Mind of Christ.

Now, as the redeemed of the Lord speak the Word of the Lord, they will be speaking with the voice of God, which is a creative voice built on the matrix of the LIFE of Christ. His spoken Word will be the audible external vibrations of the internal LIFE of Christ being spoken through the redeemed. This is the Ruach Life Breath of God.

As the redeemed vessels carrying the LIFE OF CHRIST speak, ...as HIS LIFE comes forth in the vibrations of the spoken and audible voice....., creation will take place just as when God created the Earth and all things in it.

- **THE REDEEMED BRIDE WILL KNOW.**
- **SHE WILL SPEAK.**
- **HIS LIFE WILL CREATE.**

We are told in Zachariah 4.... , ***"Speak to a mountain and it will become a plain."*** This is not figurative. This is literal. As the spoken voice of God comes forth, as the LIFE of Christ comes forth via sound with vibrations of HIS LIFE in the internal of these vessels, creation will take place and a physical mountain will become a physical plain.

This is why Romans 8 tells us the Earth is moaning and groaning, and waiting for the manifested sons of God. The vibrations of His Life coming through the voice of these people will change, create, cause life to come forth, and cause life to cease.

This voice is the voice of the governmental authority of Heaven. It is the voice of HIS LIFE, it is a voice of authority, it is a voice of creation, and it is a voice of manifestation.

It is the new voice of God that replaces the prophetic voice of God. The prophetic voice came with a wait. When a prophetic word was spoken through a prophetic voice, it always came with a season of waiting until God fulfilled His prior spoken word.

But when the redeemed of the Lord speak with His voice of Life, the Ruach Life Breath of God, the old prophetic voice that came with a wait will be annihilated and replaced with the voice of God that comes with a create .

THE WAIT is replaced with THE CREATE.

His Life is power. His Life is authority. His Life creates. His Life voice speaks the vibrations of His Life and creation and redemption come forth. His Life spreads, and takes over all life willing to surrender to the Life voice of Christ, the King of Redemption.

This voice of Life starts with Him speaking with His breath of Life in our internal. As we allow the internal breath of Life to annihilate our existence, to annihilate the existence of Jesus of Nazareth, we not only have His Life Breath voice speaking to us internally, we gain the governmental authority of His Life, Breath voice being spoken through us. The Life Breath voice progresses from not only being spoken TO us, but to being spoken THROUGH us.

This voice of Life is the ultimate voice of governmental authority. And it is evidence of His Life of governmental authority dwelling in our internal, making us vessels of Christ the King of Redemption and no longer followers of Christ or in the Christian club.

When we allow the annihilation of self and Jesus of Nazareth to the point He not only speaks to us with this Life Breath voice, but also grants us the Life Breath of God through which to speak, we are vessels of Christ, carrying the Mind of Christ and the governmental authority of Heaven. He is currently looking for the external evidence of the internal governmental authority of Heaven of Christ the King of Redemption dwelling in our internal.

This evidence is how we overcome satan by the blood of the lamb and the word of our testimony.

The word of our testimony has absolutely nothing to do with if we taught Sunday school or Bible school, or took a casserole to the church dinner. The word of our testimony has nothing to do with what we did. **FOR OUR TESTIMONY IS CHRIST THE KING OF REDEMPTION. HE IS OUR TESTIMONY.** The word of our testimony is the evidence coming forth from the internal of the voice of the governmental authority of Heaven coming from the internal Christ living in our internal place of dwelling.

A few years back he spoke an utterance that included, ***"I am choosing my Bethels. I am choosing my Bethels. I am choosing my Bethels."***

The Bethels are those in which He will dwell with His voice of the governmental authority of Heaven.

The Bethels are His vessels of Christ, the King of Redemption.

Do you see the beauty of how this works? As WE allow HIM to annihilate our remaining SELF WILL, connected to our grip on JESUS OF NAZARETH, His Life Breath voice of the Mind of Christ is the voice we begin hearing in our INTERNAL which then increases and progresses to being spoken through us into the EXTERNAL.

As this NEW voice comes forth, every mountain becomes a plain via this voice of CREATION. This new voice also speaks external annihilations whereas the process started in His Bride with internal annihilations.

His design is perfected in His Life and has been on hold until the sovereign time He has released and is moment by moment unfolding. Now being brought forth in and through His Bride to be THE VOICE of Christ for the creations and the annihilations mandatory for the Mind of Christ to be the governmental authority in the Earth. **THE TRUE ROD WHICH RULES THE NATIONS!**

COME LORD! COME!!

NOTES

Chapter 12
Internal Expressions of His Life

"What I desire above all else is that you lay aside all old ways of Me."

In this portion of the writings, I am going to include many beautiful things His Life has spoken and released in the internal that are each individual dynamics of this blind date. But when combined together they give us such a beautiful taste of Glory Divine!

Each of these expressions OF HIM are a small piece of the wholeness of Him as redemption. FOR HE IS REDEMPTION. In the prior section of these writings, we looked at definitions, or descriptions of powerful truths you will discover as you continue reading. We are now stepping into expressions of Him regarding those individual truths.

Each of these was spoken internally by His Life Breath voice. The Ruach Life Breath voice of God that resides in the internal of His Bride who are becoming "aware" of the 'move He IS making'.

The following expressions of His voice I am sharing began around 2018 and continued to the current timing of late 2025. As His Life in you grows from the seed of salvation into His Life of Redemption, you will notice how He will begin to speak internally with breaths of His Life. Each of the following are the words attached to His breaths of Life communicating in the internal. Meaning, what He releases is the Mind of Christ via HIS LIFE Breath. It's not words He once released before this move He is currently making. It's LIFE in the form of what I am calling Life Breaths.

Redemption is the release of the Mind of Christ, and because of growing more in the Mind of Christ, the Life Breaths come within the internal. These breaths are knowings from the Mind of Christ as to what He is releasing. We then attach language, words, to the knowings coming forth from the Mind of Christ via HIS LIFE BREATHS.

As I list these beautiful Breaths of Life in the format of words, some will include an explanation and some will not. I am doing it this way because I believe He will breathe in you and give you knowings from the Mind of Christ of what He has shared of Himself.

I also am not going to list the year, dates and months, of these beautiful expressions of Him. And they might not even be in chronological order. That does not even matter to Him! The matrix of each of these is His Life of Redemption, so we will begin now...

The following are a very, very small portion of what He has released. Only a few examples of beautiful things the breath of His Life has spoken in my internal. All expressions, not of Jesus of Nazareth, but of Christ, the King of Redemption.

- ***"What I desire above all else is that you lay aside ALL old ways of Me."*** (this is in reference to the annihilation of the paradigm of Jesus of Nazareth)

- ***"It is no longer about the anointing upon (a vessel), it is about the presence within."*** (a vessel) ...(the presence of Christ the King of Redemption)
- ***"Everything I tell you from here on out, will defy logic."*** (His Life Breaths defy the fallen and logical mind)
- ***"I am no longer doing everything I once said."*** (annihilating even things HE once said)
- ***"I am removing the religion, rules of what I once said, and exchanging them for the Life of who I am!"***
- ***"I am coming off the pages of the written word."***

- 💣 ***"Keep living, but stop holding onto this life and this world."***
- 💣 **"Remember Lot's wife, and do not look back!"** (Enough said! We cannot look back at the annihilations of it all or it will stop us in the tracks of the escape He has made for us)
- 💣 ***"Untethered!"*** (it is not what you own, but what you grip)
- 💣 ***"If you believe my words that defy logic, I will catapult you to the bosom."***
- 💣 ***"Time is in you."***
- 💣 ***"You can change the epochs."***
- 💣 ***"You can change the times."*** ...(the last three are Him telling us that by staying in cadence with the Mind of Christ, the time of His return is changed and comes forth)
- 💣 ***"If it looks like yesterday, it's not of me says Holy God."***
- 💣 ***"I am moving forward, and if you do not move forward WITH Me, you will lose your position IN Me."***
- 💣 ***"As I step into the internal, My Bride steps into the eternal."***
- 💣 ***"There is a respite mandatory for the becoming!"*** (We must rest IN HIM in order to become HIS READY BRIDE)
- 💣 ***"As you know what I know, speak it. And I will create it."***
- 💣 ***"Lay down and walk away from all the external DOING, in exchange for the internal BECOMING."***

- ***"Hold on to habitation for I am coming with habitation."*** (this was an encouraging Word to hold because the road seemed to be getting longer and longer)

- ***"The annihilated Christ is about to reveal Himself through the annihilated bride."***

- ***"The tide has turned. You are in the day of vengeance. Justice will be served."***

- ***"As you advance in My Life, the coupling of time will produce the combustion of redemption."***

- **"The beauty for ashes are my priest in the order of Melchizedek."**

- ***"The house is built. I have placed my seal on it. Now go and steward the house of God."***

- ***"Travail is the process of going deeper into Oneness with me."***

- ***"Keep your heart attached to Me and stay away from false expectations."***

- ***"Redemption unto the Mind of Christ is a whole New World, a new fantastic point of view, the greatest show on Earth!"***

- ***I am giving people what they believe!"*** (This is a strategic warning because He was referring to whatever we believe. If we believe the writings in this book, this is what He will grant us. If we believe nothing has changed then nothing will change. If we will believe Jesus of Nazareth remains the same, we will not be included in redemption of Christ, the King. There is so much connected to this warning! Whether what we believe is indeed what HE is doing or whether what we believe totally contradicts what HE is doing, He is giving people what they believe!)

- 💣 ***"I am honoring choices to the very end."*** (I love that one because we can make the choice even now to allow Him to annihilate self will over Jesus of Nazareth and He will honor our choice)

- 💣 ***"THIS Samuel is internal."*** (He was letting us know the internal voice of His Life does not fall to the ground. It is exactly and perfectly accurate.)

- 💣 ***"I am the Third Day."*** (The new era. The millennial reign)

- 💣 ***"We are now moving in zero tolerance cadence which will annihilate the remaining fallen mind and take you all the way into full redemption."***

- 💣 ***"I do not honor fables."*** (He is not honoring the past ways of Him)

- 💣 ***"You must remain in Heaven's perspective."***

- 💣 ***"You, my people, are at the beginning of the dawn of the new day. It is the new era that has never been seen before."***

- 💣 ***"You are at the beginning of oneness."***

- 💣 ***"I am looking for the evidence of governmental authority to manifest through you."***

- 💣 ***"Walk with Me breath by breath."***

- 💣 ***"Your position is the position of receiving annihilation...."***

- 💣 ***"The book of Revelation is on reserve for the Mind of Christ."*** (He was letting us know. The book of Revelation is only properly understood, interpreted, and lived out via the Life of Christ coming forth from the Mind of Christ. Knowings of Christ, not intellectual interpretation or historical understanding.)

You will begin to recognize the internal Life Breath voice of the Mind of Christ as you allow Him to annihilate the self will over Jesus of Nazareth. It is through His internal Life Breath voice we know the cadence, as well as the zero tolerance cadence of His focused, swift, and stern forward movement into our redemption.

I will share, the internal voice is becoming more frequent, the cadence is becoming more frequent, and the speed of each cadence playing out and being fulfilled is becoming more frequent.

I invite you to join HIS cadence of annihilations of the fallen mind of a man because the rooster is about to crow three times and we do not want to be found running, hiding, and in denial of Christ, the King of Redemption!

WE MUST KNOW HIM NOW AS THE ANNIHILATED CHRIST SO WE WILL RECOGNIZE HIM SOON!!!!

NOTES

NOTES

Chapter 13
The Death Blow of Doubt

We will not enter His Rest if we <u>remain</u> in unbelief.

Doubt is absolutely the death blow to the annihilation of Jesus of Nazareth unto the truth of Christ, the King of Redemption. And the beautiful flipside of that coin is that Christ the King of Redemption is the absolute death blow to doubt!

Throughout His word and specifically in the book of Hebrews, the negative power of unbelief is addressed, making it clear we will not enter HIS REST if we remain in unbelief, which is doubt. Redemption IS HIS REST. It is HIM, HE is rest, therefore REDEMPTION IS REST.

REDEMPTION IS HIM GRANTING US HIS SOVEREIGN REST FROM THE FALLEN AND CURSED MIND.

Can we just all stand up and SHOUT AMEN!!

Along with the book of Hebrews, one of the overall messages which is a river running throughout the entire word of God is the danger of doubt, unbelief, lack of faith, and wavering. James tells us a wavering man RECEIVES NOTHING. Not a single thing. Doubt is the consistent negative force shown in His word that robs us and stops us from all aspects of HIM. Doubt specifically robs us of the internal promise of redemption His chosen bride will carry to the Earth.

Doubt and unbelief put us in perfect alignment with satan and his kingdom of darkness. Doubt is the deadly poison that kills and totally nullifies every single thing we have learned, we have known, what He has shown us, what He has spoken to us. Every beautiful promise or revelation from Him is void when doubt resides in the internal.

Doubt kills, destroys, and brings division.

No matter how many beautiful dreams and visions we have

from God showing we are His bride, we must know they are only invitations for us to allow Him to annihilate both our existence and Him, into the fulfillment of what He has shown.

They are invitations of His perfect will. They are not guarantees of His perfect will.

We also must know it is doubt that cancels out the guarantee. Faith and belief of what He has shown in our dreams brings forth the reality of the truth of His Life in us. Doubt and unbelief seals the dreams in a vault of unattended invitations.

Doubt places us in satan's kingdom of darkness, for doubt is his mode of operation. It always has been his mode and it always will be until Christ the King of Redemption totally defeats satan in our internal kingdom.

In the garden, Eve did not just eat an apple. She ate doubt. The serpent planted doubt in her with what sounded like an innocent question of did God really say not to eat of this tree? As though he, the serpent, was inquiring of Eve to clear up his own confusion regarding what a Holy God had spoken. It was deception. He was not seeking God and His truth regarding the tree. But when he asked her that question, deadly doubt entered Eve. Satan knew exactly what God had spoken. But Eve suddenly did not. She ate the apple, and the fall of mankind took over.

The fall of mankind, we as His corporate bride are still trying to stand up from.

HELP! WE HAVE FALLEN AND WE CANT GET UP! Oh but the mercy of God! He is currently making the internal move to get us up from that fall of mankind! ONCE AND FOR ALL!

Satan still uses doubt to get us completely out of alignment with Christ the King. He uses doubt boldly and in subtle ways with every bite of the doubt apple we eat, getting us more and more out of alignment with His divine and sovereign plan of redemption.

The degree or depth of how out of alignment a person is internally/mentally which is the fallen and cursed mind of man... Is the same degree or depth of how out of alignment a person is with Christ, the King of Redemption.

Doubt is indeed the death blow to redemption. What Christ the King of Redemption is serving us to eat and drink of regarding Himself, the annihilation of self will, as well as the annihilation of Jesus of Nazareth, is a huge meal to eat. When doubt is at play in any level or arena of this annihilation of the paradigm, the annihilation of the way we think, process, and do Christ, doubt is THE poison in the process.

Doubt separates the kingdoms because doubt is from the kingdom of satan no matter what degree of doubt it is. While faith and belief are of the Kingdom of Christ. Even the faith as small as a mustard seed which can grow into a giant tree is of the kingdom of God. **The seed of doubt can be equally tiny, deceptive, hidden, but also grow into a massive tree that can completely take over the internal kingdom created to be for Christ alone.** Doubt is poison and toxic and certainly is the death blow to this annihilated non-logical process to redemption.

Doubt shows up when logic is defied by His annihilations and tries to bring the defied logic back around to logical reasoning. God is defying logic, and we need to let Him. When doubt shows up to challenge the defying of logic, it is kingdom against kingdom.

Plain and simple. Kingdom against kingdom.

When doubt has been the weapon to stop us or delay us with our readiness, repentance regarding the doubt is absolutely necessary to move us forward. Repentance is a change of heart, not a sorrow of heart.

In October 2024 the Lord said,....

"I am checking the trees for three fruits of MY LIFE and moving forward with those vessels...,

***Discernment from THE LIFE of Christ,* (which is discernment that goes beyond the gift of discernment)...,**

***Belief of the things of Me that defy logic...,* (meaning no doubt over the things of Him that defy logic)**

Internal knowings From the Life of Christ and the peace that resides with these knowings...,

For this is how I am building my kingdom."

In the above ways of which HE is checking HIS trees for fruit of HIMSELF, He is emphasizing qualification and disqualification of the time we are currently in. Our state of readiness is not based on our personal successes, nor our personal failures and mistakes. It's based on being chosen and the position He has placed us in of being chosen.

AND BECAUSE WE ARE CHOSEN, HE IS MAKING SURE WE KNOW WHAT IS HOLDING US UP, WHICH IS THE LACK OF ANNIHILATION OF SELF WILL REGARDING JESUS OF NAZARETH AND CHRIST THE KING OF REDEMPTION.

We must realize in the internal kingdom of Christ, it is HE who ordained our position of being chosen. But at this point we disqualify ourselves from His ordained and sovereign position of being chosen when we do not move forward with Him in these annihilations. We can't deceptively rest or take for granted that because we are chosen, we are qualified and counted in. This is because doubt disqualifies us from having been chosen.

To fully overcome doubt, there is a requirement that we surrender our existence for total annihilation of our stinking opinions of which WE call truth. This is vital, **BECAUSE DOUBT RESIDES IN THAT WHICH IS NOT ANNIHILATED BY HIM.** And we must let HIM exchange our doubt and opinions for THE ONE who is THE WAY, THE TRUTH, and THE LIFE.

It's worth repeating.....DOUBT RESIDES IN THAT WHICH IS NOT ANNIHILATED BY HIM!

- **He is the narrow road, not the narrow mind.**

There is no need for anyone to accuse anyone else of coming up with their own truth outside of Him, because HE is the one who came up with this crazy idea from the foundations of the Earth of annihilating what we HAVE ALL known as truth. We are blessed to be sovereignly chosen to be alive in this time to participate with Him in the restoration of all things, with all things coming in force from the truth of who HE truly was, and is, and is forever more.

He was the truth long before we inherited the cursed mind and came up with our own fallen ideas of what truth is, and who He is.

- **It is time we allow HIM to straighten it all out.**

Based on the original and complete prophecy from Isaiah 61, and Luke 4 where Jesus reads a portion but stops without reading the entirety of the original prophecy, He makes it known to all of mankind HE is coming to set the captives free. The captivity we need to be set free of more than any other captivity is the captivity of doubt. Currently, He is really and truly saying and doing what has been written in these pages.

HE IS READY AND AVAILABLE TO MOVE IN AND ANNIHILATE ALL CAPTIVITY OF THE INTERNAL DWELLING PLACE OF GOD.

I love how in Luke 4 when He reads the original prophecy from Isaiah 61, He stops short of the second portion of verse two and does not include the words of the prophecy of...

"And the day of vengeance of our God"...

This is because this portion of the prophecy from that point onward is about to be fulfilled via the governmental authority of Heaven operating in the internal of the chosen bride.

IT WILL BE HIM FULFILLING THE REMAINING OF THE PROPHECY, BUT HE WILL BE DOING IT FROM THE INTERNAL OF HIS BRIDE WHO ALLOWED HIM TO ANNIHILATE FROM WITHIN.

THE ANNIHILATIONS MUST TAKE PLACE TO MAKE ROOM FOR HIM TO HAVE A PLACE TO "LAY HIS HEAD" of AUTHORITY.

HIS READY BRIDE is about to finally cancel Him, 'having no place to lay his head'. And give Him Her internal place to lay His head. It's so beautiful and WE are in HIS sovereign time of fulfillment!

We know the true bride is called to rule and reign with Him, however, the ruling and reigning starts in the internal where we are to rule and reign with Him as truth, and with Him as the full government of Heaven over the curse of doubt. For doubt is indeed a curse and doubt is indeed captivity.

He is currently removing us from corporate captivity of doubt, so we can move forth in this annihilation, and He can have His Bride made ready.

As we rule and reign with Him in the internal kingdom and allow Him to annihilate our self will over Jesus of Nazareth, He overcomes the curse of doubt. We do not overcome anything. **It's all him, THE OVERCOMER who overcomes within us, bringing us forth as Overcomers.**

This victory of overcoming doubt is not accomplished any other way than Him increasing from the seed of salvation into the Life of Christ, where He fights for us internally in the warfare over doubt, for warfare has now moved internal. Because He is residing within His Bride, and not within the established church, warfare over doubt has now moved internal. For His true bride is the true church. Nothing more and nothing less than the true bride is the church, though much of what we participate in we do indeed call church. He died for His bride, He died for the church, meaning He died for HIS BRIDE, for His bride is the true church. And currently there is internal warfare over the true WAY, the true TRUTH, and the true LIFE versus doubt. It's kingdom against kingdom, internal warfare, where HE overcomes within us as we surrender unto the annihilations of all that is holding us back.

THE ENTIRE WAR TAKES PLACE IN THE INTERNAL AND THE ENTIRE VICTORY COMES FORTH FROM THE INTERNAL.

This is where the difference between making Him our Savior and calling Him our Lord comes into play. As Lord, He has the say-so that He is actively bonding and weaving into the internal of the bride being redeemed so that she has the say-so. When He is Lord, He takes away our opinions, decisions, and even our choices and we live through His choices, His will, His say-so. A few years back I spent close to 18 months trying to negotiate with Him over something He wanted of me. It was in hindsight I saw the situation He was placing me in was part of the annihilating of my own mind because He was about to annihilate Himself in my mind, which is the internal. And my internal had to be annihilated and palatable for the annihilation of Christ.

I did not realize that I was in rebellious negotiations with Him until the day He spoke to me and said... ***"I am requiring this of you."*** I immediately said requiring it? What about my own free will? He quickly replied, ***"well, you actually gave me your life as Lord, and this is what I am doing with it."*** That is the day I stepped into full obedience of what He was 'requiring' of me and not what I was "resisting" because He is my Savior AND my Lord. My Ruler. The ONE who has the 'say so' of what I was still calling "my life".

I share that as an example of what He is currently requiring of His true Bride, because if we are His true mature Bride, He is our Lord and not only our Savior. And He is currently 'requiring' that we allow the Life of Christ in our internal go to war over the curse of doubt ingrained in our fallen minds regarding who He really is, and what He must have from us in order for Him to come for us.

HE defeats the internal curse of doubt, *"not by might, nor by power, but by My Spirit, says the Lord."* HE DOES IT but we must humbly embrace that we are vessels of doubt way more so than vessels of His Life if we have not yet surrendered our internal existence to Him for the annihilations of our stinking self will. While refusing to even believe we must also allow Him to annihilate Jesus of Nazareth, much less actually surrender to the process of Him doing it, by His Spirit.

When we are vessels of doubt over this annihilation more so than vessels of His Life, we are also way more residing in the kingdom of satan than we are residing in the Kingdom of Christ the King of REDMEPTION.

The process of redemption brings our soul to the place it no longer sees or hears, and all seeing and hearing is done via His Life which annihilates what the soul has produced, and particularly the existence of doubt stopping us from being a bride made ready. By silencing the soul, He is exchanging the show for the know.

'Show me what you are doing', came from the soul.
'Knowing what He is doing', comes from the increase of His life, which is the Mind of Christ.

HE Is exchanging the fallen and cursed mind/soul of man for the perfected MIND OF CHRIST, when we let HIM annihilate our stinking opinions and satan's weapon of doubt out of the way.

The arena of satan is the mind of man, it is the soul, it is the unconquered, UNannihilated internal.

Christ, the King of Redemption is the conqueror who defeats satan's arena internally and all doubt flees in the name of Christ the King! When the internal kingdom is conquered by the MIND OF CHRIST, we are in perfect alignment with HIM.

We are the Ready Bride.
We are the Redeemed.

NOTES

Chapter 14
Kingdom Separation

His Kingdom Seperation is currently taking place. Now.

In this chapter titled Kingdom Separation, we are going to learn of how Christ the King is already dividing the kingdoms and bringing forth division within His own kingdom of light. I do not want you to get overwhelmed or confused regarding both the permanency of the outer court, as well as the transition of the outer court into His Bosom. This will make more sense as you continue to press through this chapter.

The difference is because of God's sovereignty of knowing the heart of man, He has already placed some of His own people permanently in the outer court, even though they have not yet passed from this Earth. I use the term Earth side. They are the ones bound to old wine skins and religious rules, though they are indeed HIS PEOPLE. They are not open to the Mind of Christ and the truth of this book.

However, I want your heart to know now as you continue to read, the outer court is also those who at this point have blind eyes and deaf ears to THIS message of the annihilation presented within this book simply due to not having yet heard this message. Due to not yet having the chance to reject or receive and walk out this message. At some point, regarding this beautiful sovereign message of the annihilation of Jesus unto Christ the King of Redemption, we all had a type of blind eyes and deaf ears to the vastness of Christ. **But because HE HAS NOW RELEASED THIS MESSAGE, as we are exposed to this beautiful truth, embrace it, walk it out, and grow in it internally, we no longer have blind eyes and death ears to this truth and HE, in His sovereign time, transitions us into His Bosom. We no longer have the blind eyes and deaf ears IF WE ALLOW HIM TO DO THE WORK INTERNALLY OF THE ANNIHILATIONS. Simply put, He must be allowed by us to take over the INTERNAL.**

We must not forget everything regarding the kingdoms is taking place internally before it bares fruit externally. The bottom line regarding the outer court as you read deeper is that you will see some are already permanently placed there. But most will not be placed in the outer court unless they reject this message FROM HIM.

Those who receive this message will transition from the outer court into His Bosom. I refer to "Earth side" because He's already making these separations as you will see in this chapter. I encourage you to hold on tight through this chapter. Do not let it confuse you or overwhelm you. I pray the Mind of Christ the King of Redemption gives you knowings from His heart of what this chapter is revealing. Please do not give up. Hold on tight and read this chapter again if needed.

As you read, you will see some are permanently already in the outer court, some are there for the chance to transition to the bosom based on this annihilating truth, and some have already transitioned into His Bosom and are growing in the vastness of Christ the King of Redemption.

The different lies in the truth that He, by His hand is already separating the kingdoms. If by His hand He has placed a person in the other court Earth side, they remain there.

But because the kingdom separation is actively taking place, those who have not been permanently placed in the outer court by HIS hand, can by His beautiful mercy and grace move into His Bosom if they allow the truth of the annihilation of Jesus unto Christ, the King of Redemption to take place in the INTERNAL.

It must take place in the internal. Reading this book 10 times will not do it for anyone. HE does the annihilation. WE do the surrendering. When we surrender to His LORDSHIP of HIS ANNIHILATIONS , by His mercy and grace, we can move from the outer court to His Bosom of REDEMPTION UNTO HIS

ORIGINAL INTENTION OF THE MIND OF CHRIST OVERTAKING THE FALEN AND CURSED MIND OF MAN.

Ok now let's progress and go deeper in this truth of the current and active Kingdom Separation.

Kingdom separation has two aspects.

❶ **The first aspect is when He separates the kingdom of light from the kingdom of darkness.** Which we could also call the kingdom of Heaven and the kingdom of hell.

❷ **The second aspect of separation is within HIS OWN KINGDOM. A separating within the kingdom of light.** Separating those who are truly His, and dividing a line between those who will reside in His Bosom as the redeemed of the Lord, and those who will reside in the outer court due to having missed redemption, yet they are still His people.

Redemption begins in the internal and expands to the external. Currently, He is already building an internal kingdom in His chosen vessels, which is actively becoming an external reality and will continue to become a deeper external reality of redemption, expressing the governmental authority of Heaven on the Earth. Expressing the divine order of His kingdom. Vessels of THE CHRIST OF REDEMPTION....HIS SECOND COMING.

Because God is indeed already bringing redemption to the internal of His chosen, this means redemption has already begun by the hand of God in this nation. It is NOT yet fully developed and manifested, but it has begun. Redemption automatically produces kingdom separation, for there can be no redemption without the outcome of separation. Redemption is HIM! Redemption is HIS blinding light! When blinding light enters darkness, it beautifully produces a scathing separation, producing the division of kingdoms.

Regarding the two aspects of kingdom separation, there is the kingdom separation where He vomits out those who are NOT HIS due to being neither hot or cold, but remaining lukewarm in hypocrisy. **Those who have pretended to be His. The hypocrites. The players. Those who participated in the shenanigans, but never connected in the heart. Those who never surrendered self to the level He was Lord, OR Savior. The separation for them is the kingdom of darkness, or the kingdom of hell.**

Kingdom separation is also, as stated above, when He divides those who are truly His people allowing HIM to be LORD, AS WELL AS SAVIOR, in their internal, soon to be external kingdom of REDEMPTION. These are the wise virgins who had oil in their lamps. These are those He calls HOT. The heart is hot and on fire for Him as Lord and Savior.

He is separating those He is redeeming from others who are His, but who will reside in the outer courts due to never allowing the internal work that was prerequisite to the internal kingdom of redemption. Due to never allowing Him to be LORD, yet they did choose Him as SAVIOR. These are the foolish virgins who had lamps, but no oil in their lamps and who also found they could not buy oil from the wise virgins because the oil represents readiness, which can not be bought or sold. These are those He calls COLD. The heart is cold due to not allowing Him to be Lord. A cold heart is invested in self rather than surrender of Lordship.

This clearly shows us the dividing factor is based on issues of non surrendered self dominance versus total surrender of self dominance. God is dividing HIS kingdom based on matters of the heart.

THIS IS BECAUSE THE INTERNAL BELONGS TO HIM AND HIM ALONE!

We all have captivity of soul. The fallen and cursed mind of man is captivity, and there are so very many levels, depths, and degrees of captivity. **We are not chosen nor disqualified based on our captivity. We are chosen and divided all based on matters of the heart.** True death of self qualifies us for internal, then later, external redemption.

Holding onto self while calling Him Savior, disqualifies redemption, but signs one up for the outer courts. While holding onto self the entire time and being a hypocrite, gets one completely removed from His kingdom and not even qualifying for the outer court, but with the outcome of the kingdom of darkness, hell.

Residing in the outer courts is not hell, but these will reside in the outer courts from this point onward, not waiting to reside there in eternity. Meaning, while His chosen vessels are already existing and increasing in the internal redemption, currently, as in NOW, the kingdom separation is also taking place even now in those who will reside in the outer courts eternally. They have already been placed in the outer courts here on Earth side, in the same way those actively being redeemed even now are already residing in His Bosom, here on Earth side. This is because HIS KINGDOM separation is currently taking place. NOW. The ear mark of recognition for the outer court are those with spiritually blind eyes and spiritually deaf ears. No matter what, they can't catch on, hold on, move forward, and continue to move forward in Him.

We all still have our feet on the ground, but INTERNALLY where the kingdom separation is taking place, we all are being divided, NOW, into the bosom of Christ for redemption, or into the outer courts for an eternal "time

out" to observe but not be included.

This is a current process, as well as an active process, meaning the kingdom separation doesn't all happen in one day or one moment encompassing the entire corporate. As His chosen vessels increase internally with the Life of Christ to the point their spirit is in proper alignment over the soul, and the vessel is operating from the completion of internal redemption, there are also those who are not increasing to the same cadence and degree, and will be separated into the outer court. Some are ALREADY placed in the eternal bosom. Some are ALREADY placed in the eternal outer court. And some are in the PROCESS of being placed in the bosom, and some are in the PROCESS of being disqualified for redemption and placed in the outer court. The kingdom transition is actively and currently taking place and will continue taking place from this time forward. Not a 'one and done deal' for the corporate as a whole. A process of individual vessels. But absolutely a 'one and done' deal once HE places an individual vessel in His Bosom or His ETERNAL outer court. (Keep reading because toward the end of this chapter there is great hope for those currently residing in the Earth side of outer court, extending great hope to transition into His Bosom) The placements by His hand are permanent placements.

The outer court is better than hell, but what a compromise caused by a lack of self surrender. Protected from hell, but not able to partake of the eternal reward. Which is the Christ of Redemption.

Some are living in the completion of internal redemption, growing and expanding into the external manifestation of full redemption.

Those of His caught up already in this kingdom separation of the outer courts have even now been placed in the outer courts to remain there, even when passing from this Earth.

And some due to matters of the heart, while still physically living on the Earth, are already residing in hell. Those He called "neither". Those not called hot, nor called cold.
The hearts of the 'neither' are invested in pride. For pride does not even remotely RESIDE in the heart which is HOT. Pride exist, but does not totally RULE the heart which is cold. And pride is KING of the heart that is 'neither'.

So the bottom line is, we have the kingdom separation where He separates the kingdom of light from the kingdom of darkness. The kingdom of darkness being those who do dwell in darkness for all of eternity, the kingdom of hell.

And, within His own kingdom of light, we have the kingdom of the redeemed and ALSO the outer court. With both sets of people already even now, beginning to live now, not waiting on what we call eternity, but beginning to live now in the internal, soon to be external kingdom of redemption. Or, the separation into the outer court, having missed the internal progressing into external redemption.

The outer court are those of His people who held onto self which included doubt regarding many things, but especially redemption. SELF and DOUBT ride tandem on the bike leading to the outer court.

BECAUSE SELF ACTUALLY IS THE EXTERNAL MANIFESTATION OF INTERNAL DOUBT.

For the redeemed of the Lord, both self and doubt have been overcome by the BLOOD OF THE LAMB, making those vessels redeemed unto HIM as Savior AND LORD.

(As you read this portion, to keep from becoming confused I

will say this... There are some already permanently placed in the outer court, but there are some who can still make it from the outer court into His Bosom by allowing Him to open their spiritual eyes and ears by THE BLIND DATE of the MISSING LINK of allowing HIM to annihilate Jesus unto Christ the King of Redemption. I am about to share regarding those who will allow Him to annihilate the fallen mind of man regarding Jesus and transition into His Bosom. WITHOUT THE ANNIHILATIONS OF JESUS, eyes will stay blind and ears will stay deaf and those will remain in the outer court. Meaning, MANY will be left in the outer court they have already been placed within.) ....

THERE IS BEAUTIFUL HOPE FOR THE OUTER COURT. NOT ONLY THE GREAT LOVE AND MERCY OF THE OUTER COURT THAT ABSOLUTELY IS NOT HELL, BUT THERE IS MORE HOPE FOR THOSE WILLING TO EMBRACE THE ANNIHILATION OF JESUS UNTO THE CHRIST OF REDEMPTION WHICH WILL CARRY THEM FROM THE OUTER COURT TO THE BOSOM OF REDEMPTION. (The outer court that remains His beautiful grace and mercy, but is an eternal time out from the reward of Christ the King, yet better than hell, is for those who never allow the internal work of the annihilation of Jesus unto Christ the King of Redemption. They will remain in the Earth side and the eternal outer court)

The outer court is full of Bride. Captive Bride who have not YET seen and heard and EMBRACED this message of annihilation of Jesus unto Christ the King. Full of the Bride who is not yet ready.

While still Earth side outer court, the captive Bride can still embrace Christ the King of Redemption.

As they transition to who He truly is, they also transition from outer court to His Bosom Earth side as well as into the eternals.

In chapter 12, titled 'Internal Expressions of His Life', it was shared He spoke the following...

"When I step into My Bride, My Bride steps into the eternals!"

When He steps into His Bride, the seed of salvation begins to grow into the LIFE of Christ the King of Redemption. As that Life increases, and increases, and increases, we step into the Mind of Christ and into the Bosom of Christ.

The established church system made by the hands of men are hubs of the outer court, and those people stay in the outer court until they get to the eternal outer court UNLESS they allow the annihilations to transition them to the Bosom of Redemption.

They stay in the outer court Earth side and enter the eternal outer courts. Or they leave the outer court via HIS annihilations of HIMSELF and enter His Bosom of Redemption.

- **THE MAN MADE ESTABLISHED CHURCH IS THE OUTER COURT.**

- **SPIRITUALLY BLIND EYES AND DEAF EARS ARE THE OUTER COURT EVEN IF NOT PART OF AN ESTABLISHED (Man made)CHURCH.**

- **REDEMPTION IS THE BOSOM.**

This truth of moving from the outer court to His Bosom is beautiful and possible because of this sovereign move HE IS CURRENTLY MAKING!!! He has already sovereignly made a way for His Bride to be with Him forever on Earth and in the eternals because the goal and reward of His sovereign move is to FINALLY HAVE HIS BRIDE IN HIS BOSOM. To have Her residing in His heart and no longer striving to figure out why He has not yet come for Her, which is the higher truth that He is coming TO HER!!

THE SECOND COMING OF CHRIST IS WHEN HE COMES TO THE INTERNAL OF HIS BRIDE WHO WILL RESIDE ON EARTH AND RULE AND REIGN WITH HIM.

This book is an open invitation to embrace the annihilation of Jesus, and move from a Bride not ready, to a Bride made ready. It is an open invitation to not squander the beautiful sovereignty of the sovereign move. For in the sovereignty, HE has made a way for you!

It is also a beautiful invitation to move from blind eyes and deaf ears of the outer court, to His Bosom of Redemption because GREAT IS HIS FAITHFULNESS!!
AND BEAUTIFUL IS HIS SOVEREIGNTY!!

COME LORD, COME!

NOTES

NOTES

Chapter 15
An Invitation To Take A Chance On Him

His plan is to bring atrophy to the fallen mind of man.

The bottom line of my crazy life the last 30 or so years and especially currently, is the profound and dominating truth that Christ is bringing us into redemption, and along the way He is annihilating the fallen and cursed mind of man so He can replace it with the Mind of Christ.

All the confusion, back-and-forth directives, telling us to do one thing and then turning around and telling us not to do it, and sometimes then telling us to do it again. Undoing things HE directed us to do and sending us in a different direction which has often been offensive to others, offensive to our own selves, offensive to religion, hard and unsettling, ...has all been for His sovereign and divine purpose of annihilating the fallen and cursed mind. **All the things we call "changes", and even "confusion" of directives are for the single purpose of making the fallen and cursed mind OF NO USE TO US.** Hence bringing the bold survivors of His annihilations into HIS original intention of creation from the very foundations of the Earth. Where we abide completely in Him dwelling in THE MIND OF CHRIST.

What has been and still is His purpose in what seems like absolute craziness? Annihilation!! He does not want us even using, turning to, relying on and certainly not depending on the fallen and cursed mind of man anymore at this point. When we do we are exercising and strengthening the muscle of the fallen mind, and therefore allowing the portion of the mind of Christ He has granted us, to begin to atrophy. His plan is the total opposite! His plan is for the fallen mind to atrophy and the Mind of Christ to be strengthened and increased via the exercises of the internal knowings of Christ. By annihilating everything He has told us and how and when He told us to do things, His plan is to bring atrophy to the fallen mind of man, therefore turning us toward the Mind of Christ, where His life, His love, and His government reside!

As HE, in HIS sovereign design cancels, changes, switches, and directs us back-and-forth, all from His own voice, we grow so weary of trying to understand with the understanding of the fallen mind, we fall in love with the knowings of the Mind of Christ and find ourselves leaving the fallen and cursed mind totally out of the process. THAT IS HOW HE ANNIHILATES! He knows exactly what He is doing with what we call changes and confusion of HIS voice.

We need to know and recall that anytime we depend on our fallen and cursed minds in desperation for understanding, we are exercising and strengthening the captivity of the minds of man while His agenda is for them to atrophy completely away and bring us to where we operate fully from the Mind of Christ, WHICH IS REDEMPTION!!

THE FALLEN AND CURSED MIND OF MAN IS WHERE WE SEEK UNDERSTANDING, BUT THE RESULT IS FALLEN AND CURSED UNDERSTANDING.

His agenda is for us to have and operate from the Mind of Christ which releases REDEEMED KNOWINGS of what HE Knows.

Intelligence is from the fallen mind of Man. Knowledge is from the mind of Christ.

When we operate out of understanding and intelligence, we are stewarding the kingdom of darkness from which the fallen mind resides. When we operate with the knowings of Christ and His knowledge, we are participating with the kingdom of light where the Mind of Christ resides.

Back in July 2025 when He said, ***"the remaining road to redemption would be a cadence of what He called zero tolerance cadence, He said the zero tolerance cadence***

would annihilate the remaining fallen mind." He showed us that zero tolerance means the fallen and cursed mind would not understand what He was saying and doing, but the cadence would be the beautiful knowings of the Mind of Christ of absolutely what HE is saying and doing.

Therefore, the zero tolerance cadence that does annihilate the remaining fallen mind and bring us directly into redemption, comes without logical understanding. It absolutely and completely defies all logic and it is the Mind of Christ replacing ALL we have ever known. Scathingly annihilating ALL WE HAVE EVER KNOWN AND DONE with Him, in Him, and of Him.

I am learning His zero tolerance cadence that annihilates the fallen mind and that beautifully opens up the Mind of Christ, very often contradicts HIS prior cadence of even what HE told us to do or not do. This is because He speaks to us based on the cadence in which we are currently abiding. When the cadence changes and we are brave enough to go forward into a deeper annihilation, the directives also change.

We must live this remaining road to redemption breath by breath, inhaling and exhaling the Mind of Christ. Doing, saying, and believing nothing from the fallen mind. The fallen mind is cursed, and it will do nothing but confuse us, invite fear, and slow us down on this path to redemption.

I still find myself hurt, saddened, and shocked at times regarding things the Lord reveals to me from the internal Mind of Christ, which is the completion of internal redemption He made me aware of in June 2025. I sometimes find myself stalling due to being grieved or stunned. Sometimes the stalling comes from wanting more understanding, when I know, that I know, that I know the Mind of Christ annihilates understanding. It annihilates everything.

It even annihilates what we were doing "yesterday" that was completely OF HIM, yesterday.

With a beautiful, bold and hard truth that zero tolerance cadence not only annihilates the remaining fallen mind, but is the cadence that gets us to the completion of redemption. We must live fully from His mind which still rocks us and shocks us, knowing that we know what He knows.

For with each gallop of His cadence annihilating our very existence to bring us fully into His existence, we find ourselves breath by breath arriving at full redemption.

The closer we get to the final and complete arrival, the more people CHRIST will remove. The final curve to redemption becomes empty and lonely right before it becomes completely full OF HIM and His corporate bride who also "took a chance" with HIM and submitted to His invitation of scathingly painful annihilations, which once suffered and survived, produce complete, total and absolute victory of Redemption in Christ, the King of Redemption!

Although it might absolutely feel like it, we are not "risking it all" to step into the Mind of Christ, and into redemption of Christ, the King of Redemption. In reality, we are receiving it all!

Everything we ever dreamed, long for, and hope for, resides IN HIM. He is standing at the altar, waiting on HIS READY BRIDE.

These writings are a beautiful invitation to go into the dressing room of the ready bride, put on the proper garments, then stoop over and grab the hem line and GIRD UP WITH HIM!

- **Get in position and remain in position.**
- **Catch up with HIM, keep up with HIM, and arrive IN HIM.**

I look forward to seeing you there. Equipped with the Mind of Christ to rule and reign WITH HIM!

NOTES

Chapter 16
Oneness With Christ The King

A <u>new</u> identity for the Bride and a new identity for the King.

All of Heaven is standing in vicious fight mode for the Bride to step into war with Christ the King of REDMEPTION over the addiction to Jesus of Nazareth.

I invite you to suit up and join all of Heaven in this fight for the annihilation of the cursed and fallen mind keeping us stuck while calling ourselves, A READY BRIDE!!

Of all people, the Bride should not be caught guilty of being self deceived that she is ready while holding onto the old and not embracing the new.

I find it very beautiful that because there is a vital requirement for the Bride to be annihilated of self, Christ the King of Redemption also annihilated Jesus of Nazareth. A death process for both the Bride and the King. A new identity for the Bride and a new identity for the King. Making us one. Without spot or wrinkle. Both annihilated. Into ONE. I just absolutely LOVE IT! He did not make this a one-sided annihilation. Because we are to be an exact representation of Him, side-by-side, equal with Him.....HE is annihilating both us and Him into ONE.

In John chapter 11, we know the famous verse of ***'Jesus wept'.*** But it is often overlooked as to why He actually wept. It is often told that He wept because Lazareth, His dear friend had died. But Jesus knew beforehand exactly how things were going to play out. And He even stated it was not unto death. He was not crying because He thought God had failed Lazarus, his sisters and Himself.

Jesus wept because the sisters of Lazarus and the entire town of Bethany did not recognize Him as resurrection power. They did not recognize Him as Christ the coming King of Redemption. To redeem Lazarus and now us from death to life.

He literally broke my heart while writing some of these chapters with a vision of Him weeping yet again over His very own Bride who should be ready by now, not yet recognizing Him as Christ the King of Redemption, and still looking for Jesus of Nazareth to come and save the day and remove the stench of Lazarus.

He wept over the town of Bethany and He is weeping over us. He wept and is weeping over the same dilemma. A lack of recognition. Yet He knows a remnant of His Bride will allow the severe annihilations of both self will of the fallen mind and of Jesus of Nazareth. So He can come for His Bride, insert His DNA of LIFE into her in His Bosom, and send her back to rule and reign with Him in the governmental authority of Heaven.

TALK ABOUT A ROD OF IRON!!!!!

The rod of iron that rules the nations IS the governmental authority of Heaven, and it is beautiful, and it is vicious and IT IS HIS READY BRIDE.

The rod of iron is the day of vengeance of our God.

We are already in the day of vengeance because vengeance means to set things straight and make things right. His vengeance is His corrections and His perfections!

He is currently setting things straight and making things right with His Bride by informing us via the Mind of Christ there is a MISSING LINK of annihilation of Jesus of Nazareth.

And, He is currently releasing the day of vengeance with a BLIND DATE of Himself to make us ready and really be ready.

For ready or not, He is about to come!

READY OR NOT, HE IS ON HIS WAY!

He knows we do not know Him as Christ the King of Redemption so He's coming to our door with a blind date of who He really is that is designed specifically, intentionally, divinely, beautifully, sovereignly, and lovingly for His chosen and mature Bride.

Can't you just see Him coming to get you? Can't you feel how nervous you are that the doorbell is about to ring for a blind date? You are about to be picked up and taken on the ride of your life with the Lover of your dreams, your soon and coming Christ the King!

I want to end this book by sharing something very personal and private with you because He has moved upon me to share it. I have shared it with a handful of people, but now it goes forward in this book of redemption. No matter which words I choose to form how I share this encounter with you, there's no way even perfected and eloquent words can do it justice. But I will try.

Oddly enough, I don't recall exactly when this happened because when it happened, I was removed from time and space as we know it. My best guess is that it was in 2022 between when He came to my bedside and spoke that ***"He was about to make this move of redemption that no one is yet aware of "*** back to the original intention of the mind of Christ. And in the timeframe before November 2022 when He said, ***"He was about to take me on a blind date."*** Somewhere in there the following is what happened...

This is what took place on a Saturday morning and what is beginning to happen to a small group on this path to redemption and what is absolutely going to happen to all of His fully ready bride who will allow Him to completely annihilate the self will over Jesus of Nazareth. This is not only going to happen to us on a Saturday morning, it's going to be our new identity. It's going to become our existence. Our 24/7 existence. It's going to be every breath we breathe. It's going to be the full internal and external expression of the Mind of Christ. It's going to be the permanent possession of His ready bride.

What I am about to share with you will be the exact representation of the Father displayed through Christ, displayed through His Bride, equally yoked to Him without spot or wrinkle in the expressions of the saviors, judges, and deliverers of Obadiah 21. Those who do the great exploits in Daniel 11. The Manifested Sons of God of Romans 8. The Bride of Christ of the book of Revelation. The Redeemed of the Lord of Psalm 107. The Manchild of Revealtion 12. The 144,000 of Revelation 7 and Revelation 14.

On a Saturday morning I got my coffee and told my husband I felt the Lord wanted me to go to the basement and have some time alone with Him. I went down and got comfortable and I don't really recall how it started, but I just began sharing with Him how I longed for Him to find His ready bride. Not long into sharing my heart with Him, the best I know to describe it is that He took me into His heart. I was not aware of leaving, going, or transitioning. **But I was extremely aware of being in a place where there were no cares, concerns, or worries. Nothing but pure love, rest, and peace. I was not aware of time. There was no awareness of any desires or needs. I did not think of anyone but Him. It was perfection within a place in Him of which I never have before or since encountered. It was peace unlike any peace I have ever known. Love, unlike any love I have ever known. And there was a quietness that was beyond a lack of sound or vibration. It was a stillness beyond and a lack of movement or even breathing. There were knowings of Christ I never knew before, nor could I recall when this encounter was over. I had no sense of touch or sensitivity to my environment, but rather I was in**

a space I don't know how to describe. To say it was amazing is an understatement. To say it was beautiful, or fantastic, or astonishing, or unbelievable, or indescribable, are all words of shortcoming to describe, share or repeat what took place.

When it was over, I did not have any sense of transitioning back to where I was before it started, but rather I was very aware I was no longer in that space. It did not leave me sad or disappointed, but it left me desperate beyond any desperation I have ever known. It left me hungrier than any spiritual hunger I had ever known.

And oddly enough, I did not realize at that moment forward I was more desperate and more hungry. But as each day came and went I noticed a drastic difference in that I had sovereignly been transitioned into a desperation that could not have been of my own making.

When I went upstairs, I was astonished that it had been over four hours since I went down with my coffee, which was now very cold and needing to be refilled.

My dear friends. My fellow Bridal brothers and sisters in Christ, what I just described is already beginning to take place in the internal of some vessels, and it is the definite and perfected existence of Christ the King of Redemption we will all soon and very soon not come in and out of, but permanently reside in and carry to a lost and dying world.

We are about to love with His love that will do more than we ever thought His power would do.

When we go to enter a room He will cross over the threshold with us and do the work before we can get both feet in the room.

It will be a love I wouldn't even dare to try to describe at this point. It will be beautifully and sovereignly perfected and coupled with confrontation to set the crooked paths straight.

- **HIS LOVE which creates.**
- **HIS LOVE which annihilates.**
- **The Spirit and the Bride say come!**

This unified cry is the pull of the Spirit responding to the cry of the Bride stepping into oneness with Christ the King!

Come Lord, Come!!!

NOTES

NOTES

Chapter 17
As He Is

When He comes we shall see Him As He Is.

First John 3:2..... "***It has not yet been revealed what we shall be, but we know that when He is revealed, we shall be like Him, for we shall see him AS HE IS."***

That one scripture hidden toward the back of our Bibles says it all. Which is this book in a nutshell. We shall see Him AS HE IS. Not as He WAS and not as we were told, not as we thought, not even as we experienced because of the limitations of the fallen mind. **But we will see HIM AS HE ACTUALLY AND TRULY IS!**

Currently, Christ the King is revealing not only what and who we shall be when He is revealed, but also who HE will be. He began revealing who He shall be when He came to the bedside in February 2022 and announced... ***"I am about to make the move no on is yet aware of."*** Then He became active with revealing who He truly is when He came in November 2022 and announced, ***"I am about to take you on a blind date."*** The blind date thus far has revealed who He is, Christ, the King of Redemption.

Ever since the fall of mankind, we have made Him logical. We have interpreted Him with our fallen minds, negotiated, renegotiated, arranged, and rearranged anything, and everything to form Him into a logical Christ to fit our fallen and logical minds. **But when He comes, we shall see Him AS HE IS! More like a Gandalf. Total disruption. Upheaval of everything that has been of Him and associated with Him.** Most will not survive the annihilation to Christ the King of Redemption. As He reveals who HE TRULY IS, we will see a civil war come forth from within the church system fighting over Jesus versus Christ the King of Redemption.

For those of us called to rule and reign with Him, we must join toes to toes, hand in hand, nose to nose, and eyes to eyes with Christ the King of Redemption to annihilate our grip on Jesus and to embrace the coming King!

In a prior chapter we have already discussed the kingdom separation. Probably two years ago the Lord asked me a question I did not understand at the time, but now I do. The question was, ***"Will you be OK if MY CHURCH does not fully embrace you?"*** I said "Well, Lord, I do not even understand how anything you call your own would not embrace you, but because of you and your internal life, I'm sure I will be OK". Now I understand what He was asking, as well as, what He was saying. He referred to the church as HIS church when He said will you be OK if MY church does not fully embrace you? Of course He was not referring to me personally. He was referring to the annihilation He has been having me teach. The annihilation of Jesus. Now through the Mind of Christ I know the church He is referring to that is indeed HIS, but yet who also does not embrace everything within this book, is indeed the outer court. Both Earth side and also on the side of eternity. They are His saved. They are truly HIS. Which is why He said MY church. **But the redeemed of the Lord, who have the 'say so', are the ones who will truly see Him AS HE IS because it will only be the annihilated bride who will recognize and embrace the annihilated Christ!**

The outer court are indeed His Bride but the redeemed are Bridal. The difference lies within the internal of us all. Do we want to continue to court Him throughout eternity, or do we want to actually marry Him and rule and reign with Him? This book is inviting you to go from the courtship of being His Bride into the marriage of being Bridal with Him.

He is a jealous God, and He is fighting for those who are Bridal while still loving His Bride. In the chapter on kingdom separation we discussed how the outer court is not the eternal reward of Christ the King of Redemption, but it is a gracious place of love and mercy for His church. Those He referred to as MY CHURCH, His Bride. They will not be in hell. But they also will not be redeemed back to His original intention from the foundations of the Earth. Nor will they be ruling and reigning with Him.

This book has been written to help you, push you, encourage you, and invite you to step from Bride to Bridal. Bride is the IDENTITY of the saved. Bridal is the POSITION of being chosen due to readiness unto redemption.

For the Bride stepping from Bride into Bridal, she steps from the seed of salvation which gives her the identity of Bride into the maturity of His Life, into a greater maturity of His Life. His Life continues to grow into an even greater maturity of His Life, that grows into the Mind of Christ, into a greater degree and increase of the Mind of Christ, and increasing more and more in His internal Life and the Mind of Christ unto full redemption.

Those Bridal, the redeemed of the Lord, will have perfect protection from the Life of Christ in the internal. The outer court, according to Revelation 11:2 is not measured (within redemption) and is left for the nations. Simply put this means protection has been lifted for the outer court. The reward is not going to hell while also being wrapped in His grace and mercy of the outer court, but the consequence is a lack of protection. The eternal timeout consequence for lack of embracing His Lordship. HIS say so over their lives.

I recall in the fall of 2023, two years ago now when He spoke to me and said, ***"Everything, I tell you of Myself from here on out will defy logic."*** Since then I have become very aware the litmus test of truth and validity of what He is now revealing of Christ the King of Redemption that has completely annihilated Jesus, is the litmus test of logic. If it defies logic, it is Christ the King!

Throughout this book, I have often referred to Jesus as Jesus of Nazareth. But I want to clarify here, I am speaking of ALL of Jesus who is being fully annihilated by Christ the King of Redemption. This includes baby Jesus. The boy Jesus. Jesus, the son of the carpenter. Jesus who began his ministry after years of preparation. Jesus who turned water to wine, healed blind eyes, confronted the religious, taught the truth in the synagogues, the man of Galilee, Jesus of Nazareth, the Jesus who had 12 disciples, the Jesus of the Last Supper, the Jesus who died on the cross, and even the Jesus who resurrected..... **Are ALL the Jesus being annihilated! The entire Jesus. All of Jesus. From the very beginning. To the very end. Annihilated by the vastness of AS HE (truly) IS.** The Christ we are just now getting to know which leads us into Christ the King of Redemption.

Did we fall in love with that Jesus? Yes we did or we would not be this far. Did He do a beautiful job even though our minds have been fallen? He did as good as a job as we allowed. But, is He now coming in with His original intention that is greater than we can even fathom? YES HE IS!!!

This is a vital part of the annihilation as we must allow Christ the King to annihilate anything attached to ALL of Jesus because it is only the annihilated bride who will recognize the annihilated Christ when HE comes for her.

DO WE WANT TO BE LOOKING UP 'FOR OUR REDEMPTION DRAWS NIGH' AND NOT EVEN RECOGNIZE HIM BECAUSE WE DID NOT FIRST ALLOW HIM TO ANNIHILATE HIMSELF??

Those not annihilated in the fallen and cursed mind of Jesus, ALL of Jesus, will see Him AS HE IS and rebuke Him due to not knowing Him, at all.

To be specific, this annihilation includes surrendering every single aspect of Jesus, to Christ the King, and allowing Him to annihilate anything we are still attached to from the

moment of His birth in a manger, to the moment He was resurrected from the dead, walked 40 days on the Earth, then ascended to seat Himself at the right hand of the Father. Anything we think, believe, participate in, hold onto, live through, are stuck in, or reside in, must be annihilated by HIS LIFE COMING FORTH FROM THE SEED OF SALVATION AND GROWING AND GROWING AND GROWING. **It can't be annihilated by reading this book or the words in this chapter. All 'traditions of men' we are still an active part of must now be annihilated BY HIS LIFE INCREASING IN THE INTERNAL OF EACH VESSEL.**

As we surrender and step into the annihilation of HIS HISTORY AND OUR HISTORY WITH HIM, He will annihilate every aspect of Jesus as long as we participate with the scathing annihilations. I cannot tell anyone to stop holding onto any aspect of Jesus, Christianity as we have known it, the established church system, the songs we sing, the books we read, the things we celebrate, etc. **The process must be one in which HE by way of HIS LIFE in the internal comes forth and annihilates.** I have learned that as He annihilates I become very aware internally of the aspect of Him which He is annihilating. When we become internally aware He is annihilating an aspect of Jesus, we must participate in that annihilation and not just say, "oh, that's what you're after now". We must engage with Him and participate in the internal agitations alerting us of His annihilations and this is why...

EVERY SINGLE ASPECT REGARDING ALL THE ABOVE JUST MENTIONED OF JESUS AND ASSOCIATED WITH JESUS GETS US CLOSER AND CLOSER TO FULL MANIFESTED REDEMPTION. BOTH INDIVIDUALLY AND CORPORATELY.

EACH ANNIHILATION GETS US CLOSER TO A BRIDE MADE READY. TOTALLY AND COMPLETELY READY.

I am going to share some examples of what we must allow HIM to annihilate, but this is a very limited list. I believe it will help open our fallen minds to the Mind of Christ.

I am referring to THEY as churches, and ministries. I am referring to CHRIST as Christ the King of Redemption, not Jesus.

THEY ARE SAYING STAY IN CHURCH OR GO BACK TO CHURCH AND LEARN MORE OF JESUS.

- ***CHRIST HAS SAID JESUS IS NOW A FABLE. A MYTH. TURN TO CHRIST THE KING OF REDEMPTION.***

  THEY ARE SAYING REGARDING THE CHURCH SYSTEM, AND THE GOVERNMENT OF THIS NATION, THAT WE SHOULD MAKE THINGS BIGGER, REBUILD, RESTORE, COMEBACK STRONGER.

- ***CHRIST IS SAYING, ANNIHILATION, ANNIHILATION, ANNIHILATION.***

  THEY ARE SAYING BUILD THE GOVERNMENT BACK STRONGER.

- ***CHRIST IS SAYING HE IS GOING BACK TO THE DECLARATION OF INDEPENDENCE AND GOING TO UNDO IT ALL IN ORDER TO BRING IN THE GOVERNMENT OF HEAVEN. HE IS SAYING HE MUST COMPLETELY ANNIHILATE THE GOVERNMENT OF OUR NATION.***

  THEY ARE SAYING GROW INTELLECTUALLY BY LEARNING ALL YOU CAN. (THEY ARE SAYING INTELEC).

- ***CHRIST IS SAYING HE IS ANNIHILATING THE INTELLECTUAL MIND OF MAN AND BRINGING IN THE***

MIND OF CHRIST, WHICH IS TRUTH. (HE IS SAYING TRUTH).

THEY ARE SAYING WE MUST HAVE EXTERNAL WORLD PEACE.

- ***CHRIST IS SAYING HE IS PEACE, BUT UNTIL HE COMES WITH REDEMPTION, THERE WILL BE INTERNAL WARFARE.***

THEY ARE SAYING, BIGGER, BETTER, LARGER AND STRONGER BY THE HANDS OF MAN.

- ***CHRIST IS SAYING THAT HE IS CALLING OUT A VERY SMALL REMNANT OF HIS BRIDE TO BE BRIDAL WITH HIM.***

THEY ARE GLORIFYING MAN, THE GOVERNMENT, AND THE CHURCH SYSTEM.

- ***CHRIST IS SAYING TO GLORIFY HIM ONLY.***

THEY ARE SAYING REVIVAL, REVIVAL, REVIVAL.

- ***CHRIST THE KING IS SAYING REMNANT, REMNANT, REMNANT.***

The more HE annihilates ALL of Jesus and the more that comes forth of Christ the King of Redemption, truth grows bigger and larger, and more powerful rather than truth dying away. **This is because Christ the King of Redemption is the Christ of the original intention of God from the foundations of the Earth we never got to know until the gracious and beautiful invitation of the 'Blind Date, The Missing Link To Bridal Readiness.'** While on this blind date, we will continue to learn of the vastness of who HE really is and always has been. And the vastness of the TRUTH of who HE IS.

If we picture this truth as a massive oversized lion, we can see how easy the truth of Christ the King is indeed a massive and oversized lion! Yet those with blind eyes and death ears, those in the outer court as well as the religious will look at this massive lion and not even recognize a lion, but will see a deer. They will try to hunt and shoot and kill the deer. They will stare at the massive lion and insist it was and still is a deer. A deer that was alive, which they shot, which they believe is now dead. They will never be able to see that not only was it a lion all along, that grew to a BIGGER LION and never a deer, they will not even be able to see they didn't kill it because they were not ABLE to kill it. While all along it was and is and forevermore will be a massive lion not dead at all. The deception will keep them from seeing the lion and continuing to call it a deer, and that same deception will call it dead and not able to see that it is VERY alive! The vastness of 'AS HE IS' will do nothing but increase throughout all of eternity. Not able to be killed by the religious naysayers. It will grow and grow and grow as we step deeper and deeper and deeper INTO HIM AS HE IS!

That is how deception is produced from the fallen and cursed mind that insist on logic and will not take the chance with Christ the King of Redemption to defy all logic of HIMSELF.

Revelation 1:8..... "*I AM the Alpha, and the Omega says the Lord God, the one who IS, and who WAS, and who is TO COME, the Almighty.*"

Revelation 1:5....The one who WAS, based on verse 5, washed away our sins with His blood.

Revelation 1:6.... The one who IS, based on verse 6, is making us to be a kingdom and priest to serve God the Father forever and ever amen.

The one who IS TO COME, based on verse 1:8.... Is Christ the

King of Redemption. Encompassing both the Alpha and the Omega. Encompassing the one who IS, and who WAS, and who IS TO COME, the Almighty King of Redemption!!

I love how HE reveals to us in those verses there is a change from He who WAS, He who is, and He who is to come and is currently coming! He let us know in the full sovereignty of His existence what He is NOW doing. He Himself revealed He was a 'HE WHO WAS'. Past tense. A HE who WAS.

He is very actively in the process of going from being the cornerstone into being the capstone. We must tap into His VASTNESS and keep going deeper, and deeper, and deeper, for ALL of eternity. We must leave the logical and the limited behind and reside forevermore in the vastness of Christ the KING. He is looking for us to grant Him the seat of prominence and preeminence in the internal. He is to be glorified in the whole Earth. He is to be glorified in HIS vessels.

So where did all the content of this book come from? It came from HIM. From HIS LIFE INTERNAL. HE is the LIVING WORD.

He is THE WAY, THE TRUTH, and THE LIFE.

The LIVING WORD is HIM,

- **HE is the <u>WAY</u> of redemption.**

- **HE Is the <u>TRUTH</u> of redemption.**

- **HE is the <u>LIFE</u> of redemption.**

ALL are found IN the LIVING word of the LIFE of Christ, within the internal of the annihilated vessel, the KING OF REDEMPTION.

COME, LORD! COME!!

NOTES

A Final Word Of A Loving Warning

To my fellow Bride. I have never had nor do I currently have a desire to write and publish a book. This has been done quickly because the internal Life voice of Christ the King of Redemption has instructed me to do so. This book is only a small fraction of what He has released. He has instructed me to withhold most and to share enough to get His urgent points across. His point that the Bridegroom is on His way and weeping over the lack of readiness. He is indeed on His way and He is very close.

My warning is His warning. And it is a warning of complacency. He is not coming for a complacent bride. He is coming for a ready bride. He is laying on my heart to add this final page to share with you. This small book is an urgent invitation from Him. It is an urgent invitation to surrender the deep area of self which is the self will of what we think He's going to look like and how we think He's going to do it. The self will of who we think He has chosen and who we think He will choose. The self will over the annihilation of Jesus of Nazareth. Self will over qualifications and disqualifications of those we approve of and those we do not approve of.

Because just as it was with King David, man looks at the outer appearance, but God looks at the heart.

He is lining up the hearts and about to call names.

The warning is in that because there is genuinely a small

corporate group who are actively living, breathing, and walking out the completion of internal redemption that is growing into the manifestation of external redemption, qualifying at this point to be chosen and included as a ready bride is going to require desperate repentance regarding not yet being ready and a desperate plea for Him to hold on a little longer before He draws the line in the sand of the READY BRIDE versus the WAITING BRIDE.
The line in the sand between the wise virgins and the foolish virgins.

I had no intention of adding these last pages, but I am very aware the kingdom separation shared in chapter 14 is already taking place. Do not let this warning disqualify you by assuming it's too late. Let this warning be what it is. Let it be straight from the heart of Christ the King for the last call for alcohol, so to speak.

He is specifically intentional with every word He speaks, and everything He does. And when He spoke in the internal a few years ago...

"When I step into the internal, my bride steps into the eternal"...

He was giving us a beautiful kiss of the dynamic of the entire beautiful plan of redemption. All summarized in those simple yet powerful words. **As HE steps into US, WE step into the ETERNAL OF HIM.**

He is bringing His Bride into perfect divine order with Him as the head of each individual bride, making up His corporate bride in divine order with Him. And in doing so, ...He is taking fallenness off of divineness, because divine order is not fallen.

There must be a deeper surrender unto Heaven's strategy of

divine order. It is a surrender of frail human strategies and efforts, so his divine and sovereign strategies can come forth.

Hence, THE BLIND DATE.

His ways are indeed higher than our ways. And His thoughts are so very much higher than our thoughts. Let's rise together with HIM into His higher ways and His higher thoughts our fallen and cursed minds have kept us from rising into.
I look forward to seeing you there with HIM in perfect glorified REDEMPTION OF THE MIND OF CHRIST!

Keep climbing, step, after step, after step after step. Climb, climb, climb. Repetition, after repetition until you meet Him at the altar. He is there waiting on you!

THE FALLEN MIND DOES NOT STAND A CHANCE AGAINST HIS LIFE. IT MUST SUBMIT!

It boils down to, will WE believe HIM in regards to what HE is saying of HIMSELF?

LOOK UP! FOR YOUR REDEMPTION DRAWS NIGH!

Come, Lord, Come!!!

NOTES

www.ingramcontent.com/pod-product-compliance
Lightning Source LLC
LaVergne TN
LVHW020717110826
845149LV00012B/2298